PLAIN
SPEAKING

THE ATTACK ON
THE AMERICAN MIDDLE CLASS

TERRENCE WHELAN & THOMAS WHELAN

ISBN: 1466478446
ISBN-13: 9781466478442
Library of Congress Control Number: 2011960026

CreateSpace, North Charleston, SC

Preface

This book, Plain Speaking, is directed at the fourth branch of government, as set out by the American Constitution—the electorate, the citizens of the United States. It is called Plain Speaking because it will not use language that is "politically correct." The content of the book is directed at the men and women who make up the fabric of the country we call America, but without doubt it will have application to every person on Earth who longs to live in a free society and who feels powerless to make the changes necessary to see that kind of society where they live. It is a book about bravery, honor, fierce loyalty, and love. It is a story about everyday Americans working to better their families, their communities, and their nation. But it is a tale of a people who have been marginalized, betrayed, and kicked to the curb by the very institutions their forefathers set up to make them free.

This is the story of how the electorate still believes in their Constitution even when their government ignores it. It is a tale of their amazing intelligence, courage, and determination to engage in that "pursuit of happiness" that is their birthright. It is how Americans are coping with the globalization of their economy, the corruption of their political parties, and the attempt to make them twenty-first century serfs to the new world order of multinational corporations, elitist politicians, political religions, and corporate media. It is a truth seldom heard; wisdom generally ignored. This book is a letter to you about your situation and how it got this way. As you have heard many times, this country is made up of people who came here to make a better life or are the descendants of people who did so. For many it meant economic freedom, an escape from serfdom and a society that didn't allow anyone to better their lot in life, which was determined on the basis of their ancestral position. For many others it meant religious freedom, an escape from places that forced all to worship their Creator in a prescribed way. And everyone who has read the Declaration of Independence, the Bill of Rights, and the Constitution knows that when this nation was established, our Founding Fathers repeatedly stressed these freedoms and declared them to be "rights." Now strange as this will sound, not everyone believes in these freedoms nor thinks them to be a good thing. Not everyone likes our democratic process. Really, they don't.

The Elite like class societies and state religions. They want to take your labor and your money for themselves, and they don't want you to have any means to get it back. They want to tell you who to worship, how to worship, and how to live your life, and if you don't follow their rules they want the government to punish you. These people would not describe themselves as nonbelievers in democracy. In fact many loudly proclaim their great love of this country; it is not by their words, though, but by their actions that will reveal them for what they are.

It was Ben Franklin who said, **"Any society that would give up a little liberty to gain a little security will deserve neither and lose both."** These are prophetic words; in the aftermath of 9/11, politicians rushed to use this attack on America as the excuse to gut the Bill of Rights and take away the very foundations of the society they then asked

Americans to defend. Had Osama bin Laden invaded and captured the country, he could not have accomplished more than our politicians accomplished in destroying the underpinnings of our democracy. Yet they went further, attacking Iraq, a country that was one of the few secular governments in the Islamic world on the lie that they held weapons of mass destruction and were somehow involved in 9/11. The two political parties that run this country have become so corrupt that they believe they can do anything and get away with it. They are so sure of your apathy and ignorance that they have no fear of retribution. Their systematic undermining of our education systems, distortions of our news media, and collaboration with our enemies have made them confident that we are too stupid, too uninformed, and too economically ground down to stop them.

This book is written to you, the key to our collective future, and the fourth branch of government under our Constitution, to wake up and stop behaving like donkeys. That's right, not sheep, but donkeys. Sheep graze all day and the shepherd watches over them to protect them; donkeys bear the burden of the workload all day in the boiling sun and then are given the smallest amount of grasses and grain possible to keep them working another day. Unlike in the 1960s when we were a "Nation of Sheep," according to author William J. Lederer, today we are a "Nation of Donkeys," working for an elitist group of taskmasters determined to keep us going with the fewest provisions possible so they can maximize their profits and secure their hold on everything.

The amazing part is the Elite have convinced many of the donkeys that the status quo is to their benefit. It is our goal to get the donkeys behaving like men and demanding their rights under the Constitution. These rights are your birthright (or your rights through naturalization) and belong to you.

It is not our goal to ferment any kind of violence or subversion; it is true we have a long and difficult task before us to gain back our rights, liberties, and a future as a free people, but we will never get to our objective if we stoop to using violence. We must take our lessons from those who have shown the way, like Martin Luther King, Jr. and Mahatma Gandhi. These brave and dedicated men won victories for their people; sadly they did not live to share in that victory. They are success stories, and we must emulate them if we wish to know success too. Actually, these men represent the way that change is truly accomplished. Look at all the attempted violent takeovers of entrenched governmental systems and notice how many of them have failed. The ideas expressed here follow the Constitution and support constitutional means for change. If we accomplish the goals of this book, we will not need to resort to any sort of violence and we will have returned the gifts of liberty, justice, and fidelity that our forefathers intended to their rightful place upholding the Constitution. We will offer suggestions and methods to fix the problems created by our lack of vigilance as part of each chapter. So the journey to restoring our American way of life begins.

Contents

Chapter 1
Political Parties

Back in 1794 when George Washington realized that the members of his cabinet and, indeed, his closest military companions were in significant disagreement over which path the country should take and were forming political parties to promote their views, he became alarmed and warned them, saying,

I have already intimated to you the danger of parties in the state, with particular reference to the founding of them on geographical discriminations. Let me now take a more comprehensive view, and warn you in the most solemn manner against the baneful effects of the spirit of party, generally.

The alternate domination of one faction over another, sharpened by the spirit of revenge, natural to party dissension, which in different ages and countries has perpetrated the most horrid enormities, is itself a frightful despotism. But this leads at length to a more formal and permanent despotism. The disorders and miseries, which result, gradually incline the minds of men to seek security and repose in the absolute power of an individual; and sooner or later the chief of some prevailing faction, more able or more fortunate than his competitors, turns this disposition to the purposes of his own elevation, on the ruins of Public Liberty.

The common and continual mischief of the spirit of party are sufficient to make it the interest and duty of a wise people to discourage and restrain it. It serves always to distract the Public Councils, and enfeeble the Public Administration. It agitates the Community with ill-founded jealousies and false alarms; kindles the animosity of one part against another, foments occasionally riot and insurrection.

This warning is at once profound and prophetic. We are now faced with the task of responding to the warning or watching the prophecy come to pass. I think it unwise to dismiss any advice from George Washington; he was more than the general who led the Continental Army during the Revolution: he was the man who presided over the Constitutional Convention and who became our first and only president elected by acclamation. Please go back and reread the above quote from our Founding Father, particularly the last paragraph. Could anything be more prophetic?

Washington absorbed, and later came to personify, what was called the dignity code; we would understand this as an honor code. The code was based on the same premise as the nation's Constitution—that human beings are flawed creatures who live in constant peril of falling into disasters caused by their own passions. Artificial systems have to be created to balance and restrain their desires.

The dignity code commanded its followers to be disinterested in personal gain—to endeavor to put community interests above personal interests, to be reticent—to never degrade intimate emotions by parading them in public, and to be dispassionate—to distrust rashness, zealotry, fury, and political enthusiasm.

The specter of political parties becoming elitist and corrupt has been with the nation almost from the moment it was formed. It is certainly not new to our generation. Our history is the record of political parties' excesses, corruptions, demagoguery, and forceful descent toward an oligar-chy of the wealthy and privileged, as in a ruler class.

We observed political parties making laws to benefit their supporters and disadvantage their enemies almost from the very first sessions of Congress. We saw them de-clare war on various states to enlarge the geographical area of the original thirteen colonies; we saw them grab land from the indigenous populations to enrich their followers; we watched as they made the robber barons wealthy on the backs of the immigrants who came to get some of that free-dom and became the labor needed for the expansionist dreams of the wealthy industrialist. Any objective observer would see that the continuing and always existent Politi-cal–Financial Complex has trumped the Military-Industrial Complex a thousand times over, yet this is never mentioned in our "free" press.

The electorate is kept in place by a well-orchestrated system of lies and half-truths aimed at nothing less than the original political principle of divide and conquer. If you ever wondered how Hitler could have taken over a country of highly educated people who had entered into the indus-trial age with many advantages and who could have seen a very prosperous future, he did it exactly as he described in his book "Mein Kempt: tell the people a lie big enough and long enough and they will eventually believe it. That is how he got the Germans to believe that all their problems were created by the Jews. With a handy scapegoat, he could justify the complete denial of all civil liberties. Does that sound familiar? Do you remember the lead up to the Iraq War #2 and the Weapons of Mass Destruction lie? Anyone care to discuss the Patriot Act?

It is not permitted that anyone, including the president of the United States, dismiss the Constitution, yet not only did George Bush dismiss the Bill of Rights in the Constitution while he was president, he did it with the full consideration and consent of the Congress. Every bit of this political chicanery was done illegally. The only way you can dismiss a provision of the Constitution is by a vote of the states or by a Constitutional Convention. Both the president and the Congress acted illegally to take away your rights. The check on this is supposed to be the Supreme Court: their job is to reject the claims of politicians and uphold a government of law under the premises of the Constitution. That didn't happen, and it doesn't happen because—like everything else in this country—the Supreme Court has been totally politicized. Not really very surprising considering how partisan the process has become between the two political parties. The judges have to be members of the American Bar Association, they must be either strong conservatives or strong liberals, and they must be in complete servitude to the political party that nominated them. Absolutely none of those criteria were ever thought of by the Founders of this country, and certainly none of them are in the Constitution. The concept of the original Supreme Court existed in common law. The British court system with its appointment of persons to the court system based on their ancestry, not their skill, is the actual model of our current court system. But the original Founder's were never able to get the public to see that a court system that was modeled after the British system was not in keeping with the new democratic ways they had established. So they got a lot of pushback when they attempted to limit court appointments. But they definitely did not like it and said so on many occasions. They also thought it had too much power for an unelected position. Most certainly it cannot be, nor was it ever thought to be, a lifelong appointment by our Founding Fathers. It is to our detriment that they did not succeed in convincing the citizens of that particular vision.

Had the original concept for choosing judges been followed, we would have seen men like Dwight D. Eisenhower, George W. Marshall, Albert Einstein, Dr. Martin Luther King, etc. not these American Bar Association sanctioned do-nothings who have no leadership credentials or any standing in the community of this nation. This party-generated system of incompetent hacks is completely wrong, and it has given us no end of suffering and loss. It will not cease to give us suffering and loss until we change it forever. We can have no greater cause for our nation than to eliminate the influence of political parties from our land and our vocabulary. We will never see a united America until we do. We will not have real leadership until we do. The idea of a career politician was completely alien to our Founding Fathers, they could not conceive of a person wasting his life on politics and they could not think that anyone would want to spend all their time in political debate; to most of them it was an annoyance and a necessary evil, but not a lifelong pursuit. Of course that kind of thinking changed when we embraced political parties into our revolution.

It seems, and it is quite unexpected, that the electorate has become very naive in regard to the actual use of demagoguery to influence them. As George Bernard Shaw said, "But though there is no difference in this respect between the best demagogue and the worst, both of them having to present their cases equally in terms of melodrama, there is all the difference in the world between the statesman who is humbugging the people into allowing him to do the will of God, in whatever disguise it may come to him, and one who is humbugging them into furthering his personal ambition and the commercial interests of the plutocrats who own the newspapers and support him on reciprocal terms." The term "humbugging" has fallen out of style, but I'm sure you get his meaning—deliberately misrepresenting the truth.

Though some demagogues use lies, skilled ones often need to use only special emphasis by which an uncritical listener will be led to draw the desired conclusion themselves. Moreover, a demagogue may well believe his or her own arguments. (For example, there are good reasons to assume that Adolf Hitler—certainly one of the most successful demagogues in history—sincerely believed his own anti-Jewish diatribes.) Strom Thurmond undoubtedly believed his own ignorant rhetoric on racial differences between white and black. Belief doesn't make truth.

Demagogues like Rush Limbaugh, Bill O'Riley, Shane Henratty, and Nancy Cole have added a refinement to the basic diatribe: code words, unexplained and undefined, are used to let the audience know they are really agreeing with them in their racism, bigotry, and blame game mania. Devotees willingly suspend any critical analysis of the words spoken because they have sought out the speaker to get confirmation of their own convictions. Once listeners get the satisfaction of hearing their own opinions aired, these demagogues, can lead them anywhere they want to go. Recently the demagogues of the Tea Party have been determined to undermine the presidency of our first black president, and they have the ear of every racist in the country that wants the same but is trying to cloak his thoughts with the respectability of political differences, not old-fashioned bigotry. Meanwhile the liberal left wing is busy defending Army whistleblower Bradley Manning; he is due to make his first court appearance at a pre-trial hearing on December 16th. Manning faces up to life in prison for allegedly leaking thousands of diplomatic cables that were published by WikiLeaks. The fact that his actions endangered fellow soldiers serving on the front lines and caused many important in-country contacts to be targeted by the Taliban seems to not matter to this group. Manning took an oath, just like all military members to defend the Constitution, he is not a hero because he decided to betray his fellow soldiers and undermine his country.

The severely unbalanced distribution of wealth that is present in the economic figures presented later in this book naturally follow from the unlimited lobbying power of the financial institutions and big corporations who maintain 30,000 lobbyists on K Street in Washington, D.C. Now we see that the Political-Financial Complex is moving toward an elitist system that, if carried to its logical outcome, will denigrate all of us to the class of serfs. This is the inevitable outcome of lawmaking that exists for, and solely for, the benefit of big corporations. We have become the nation of the corporation, for the corporation, and by the corporation. If you don't think there is anything wrong with that, I would advise you to close this book now; nothing I say will have any impact on you. If you do see that this is wrong, read on. We need to remember that our representatives have taken an oath under our Constitution to represent us, the people of their districts, yet time and time again we see them vote to increase our burdens while making sure their friends on Wall Street have no burdens at all. Even when the whole house of cards collapses on their heads, as it did in October of 2008, they still, eighteen months later, had made no effort to apply even the smallest of reforms. So who do they represent? Not you.

If the government no longer represents the interests of its constituents then do we have a representative democracy? I think not. Does that government still have the moral authority of the Constitution?

During the debate for the prescription drug benefit to be added to Medicare the Republicans added an amendment to make it illegal for the Department of Health and Human Services to negotiate a price for those same prescription drugs; it was at Kentucky Senator Mitch McConnell's insistence that this heinous provision was passed. Remember it was a Republican-controlled Congress at the time. Now McConnell represents a state were economic disadvantage is rampant, yet who did he represent when the chips were down—the pharmaceutical companies. For that matter who did the majority of senators and congressmen who voted for this bill and provision represent? It was not you or me.

It is interesting to note that the provision stands; no one in the Democratic Party has tried to change it. But who pays for this year after year after year? It is the fourth branch—the taxpaying citizens of this country.

It is always you who pays for it—no one else, but you. When your Congress passes laws to advantage a company over its competitors, when is gives tax credits to ship your job overseas, when it allows the drug companies, the phone companies, the oil companies, the credit card companies, the mortgage brokerages, the utility companies, and anyone with a buck to bribe them gouge you, and then turns around and raises your taxes to boot, you have to know that you are the number one prey animal in this game, and every predator on the planet has been given license to hunt you by your government—who also hunts you. What an amazing system we have developed, all the while talking about the land of the free and the home of the brave. Your right as a citizen to "pursue happiness" rings as hollow as a dime store drum.

We have perhaps one of the most inefficient bureaucracies of any nation on Earth precisely because we have allowed our governmental organizations to be populated by political hacks, lawyers, and ne'er-do-wells that attach themselves to the political parties. It is very embarrassing when the president tries to send aid to either an internal disaster like the Hurricane Katrina debacle or when we send it to a foreign country like Haiti and see how completely unprepared and unorganized they are. Why? Because these government agencies are run by the parties' political hacks, which by definition are among the most incompetent citizens we have. If they weren't incompetent, they would be running their own businesses and not seeking political jobs by gaining the favor of some politician.

I need to say here that the citizens, your fellow citizens, who come to work and do their best for these agencies every day, are not the problem. They work, they are honest, they did not get their job by whom they knew, but by passing a competitive test for the position. The problem is in who is telling them what to do. Don't take this out on hard-working people who are trying to serve the public: go after the system of cronyism that allows the useless and dogmatic to make the policy for and operate these agencies. The American people have been demanding for over two hundred years that the civil services of this country be cut loose from the political apparatus and allowed to operate as any business would with the best and the brightest being promoted to the top managerial spots. That has never happened, despite the many acts that Congress has passed. How long are we going to allow this disgrace to go on?

Yes, it is embarrassing to say I am an American at these times. And why should that be the case when, after all, it is our country that is trying to step into the breach and make a difference. We should never be embarrassed by our collective desire to help others. We must get to a system in which competent, proven, trained managers run the Washington bureaucracies. By the way, if you think a citizen should never question his government or be embarrassed by its actions, I suggest you move to China; that government would love for you to be a citizen there. In the United States we must achieve a body politic that has the good sense to question everything—every attack ad especially: ask who paid for it, how does the candidate get enough money to keep running those ads, and why aren't we discussing the real issues instead of these red herring issues. We have to get to a system of governance that is led by the wise and the compassionate, not the greedy and power hungry. This can only happen when we get rid of the two political parties.

Now how do we organize and conduct a government without political parties? We wouldn't be asking that if we hadn't gone down this wrong road that our Founders asked us not to follow. This is like asking, "How are we ever going to survive if we don't keep offering blood sacrifice to the gods?" All you have to do is stop and find out what happens. We might be surprised at how quickly the old wounds heal and how rapidly we start thinking in terms of a national character instead of a political character. We might get away from the blame game and start actually fixing the problems. We do not need political parties for anything. And, by the way, neither does the rest of world. What we need are uniting structures not divisive structures. What have we gotten from representative democracy anyway? We have a national state that is run solely for the benefit of the big banks and financial institutions, a government that does not even understand the concept of political representation—only the concept of political payback. We have a nation-state that has grown so arrogant and oppressive to the rest of the world that we Americans can be sure that wherever we travel we will be hated, a nation that has completely lost the ideals of liberty and freedom, and looks more and more like a police state. We have a population that has become so disenfranchised that not even half of the electorate bothers to vote, a country so dependent on the jobs generated by the oligarchical industries that pervade it that the population is reduced to serfs for the big corporations. We have a country that daily sacrifices its most innocent and vulnerable citizens—its children—to the dictates of making a living and keeping jobs that these mighty companies command.

We have a citizenry that now has no idea of what heritage it has because its school system demands math and science, but not civics and history. We have a politicized atmosphere that has worked to keep its citizens ignorant while making sure it also keeps them divided and distrustful of each other; a system that only occasionally gives the people what they are due and then tries to make it look like a gift coming down from the elitist gods on high. We have a country so focused on playing the role of the big leader internationally that it has spent nearly every available dollar on maintaining a military and a diplomatic presence in every part of the world, to the detriment of its own citizens—especially if those citizens who are in that military. We have a country that has a justice system that would rather capture and imprison a father for stealing a loaf of bread for his children then even suggest that a Wall Street brokerage that took the retirement funds of millions and gambled them on made up debentures with no sane financial structure, were crooks.

We have a prison nation that now has 2 million people in jail for violating the hundreds of thousands of laws its lawyer representatives have made to ensure they will always have financial opportunity, even while they cannot find a law to stop the bankers from taking advantage of its citizens; like anti-usury laws capping the interest rates and limiting fees and commodity speculation. No, they can't make those laws, but they can arrest you when you protest their greed and their arrogance; we have a country whose judges invest in prisons to make money and then refuse to review sentencing of innocent people just so they can keep those prisons full. We have a country that has allowed every media outlet to be owned by corporate conglomerates: radio, television stations, newspapers, and magazines, even internet access, so they can make money on advertising their seldom-needed products, and assure themselves that the serfs never hear the truth about anything. The consolidation of media in the hands of men like Rupert Murdoch (a Australian living in Briton), and the Viacom Corporation is a serious threat to the free expression of information and truth in our society, a single corporation owning 61 stations and controlling the news you hear and the truth you believe is completely off the page as far as maintaining a free and open society. We are, and we will, pay a very high price to our liberties for allowing this to go on, it must be stopped and it must be stopped now. The Federal Communications Commission (FCC) is charged with keeping the airwaves free and not allowing the consolidation of information in just a few hands, but like everything the two political parties get control of they have been directed by their resident political crony to look the other way and allow the destruction of yet another bastion of our freedoms – a free press. Again, as in every part of this discussion the answer is not to have the government own the media, that is counter intuitive and completely ridiculous. The answer is always to move the centralization back to diversification. We need and must have community control in our media, media cannot be some international conglomerate telling you what they want you to know. It has to come back to the community and be owned by members of the community, or you will surely forfeit your freedoms and your liberty.

If you think that is the system our forefathers had in mind for their progeny and for all who would come after them, then all I can say is that you are a part of the problem not part of the solution. But I couldn't say that you are self-deceiving because you are not. What I just listed is everything you have been taught to expect from your country since your birth, including from the education system. But it is not what the Founders of this country had in mind for you. So, fellow citizen, do not think you are alone if you think this America we live in is supposed to be like it is; you are among the majority of its citizens.

What forces have created this modern America that our ancestors would abhor and even fight against? Do greed, privilege, the idea that you deserve more than your fellow citizens mean anything to you? Does the belief that elitist should rule while the peasants do the work strike a chord with you? Do you understand this country was built on the collectively focused effort of all of it's' people? Do you even realize that the basis for these elitist ideas is rooted in European class structured societies, which set your limits from the moment you were born until the day you died according to what class you were in, the very thing the country was created to thwart? Do you know that many of those European class societies came down in the revolutions of 1848? Does history tell you anything except that elitist, class-structured societies will always collapse of their own oppressive weight? Even God in the Bible forbade the Israelites from forming governments with kings and aristocracies, but they defied him and founded the Kingdom of Judah with Saul, David, and Solomon. And, of course, it fell to internal revolution even before its enemies could destroy it. The enemies only did a mopping-up exercise. Might be a good thing to re member if you think this republic is going to survive the current state of affairs.

The truth is that if you were not represented at all you would be much better off than you are now. While I'm at it, I'll add that we do not need representative democracy— we need pure democracy—we need it now because those whom you elect to represent you are not, in any way, representing your interests. They represent the people who want to exploit you, abuse you, and enslave you. How screwed up is that? The rise of the elitist class with its accompanying royalty is not new to the twenty-first century; it wasn't new in the twentieth century nor the nineteenth century. It started practically from the day the new republic drew its first breath. It has ever been and probably will ever be a symptom of European society to breed individuals who have a need to be better than their peers. This cultural inheritance has diminished the potential and the promise of our experiment in universal suffrage, unlimited democratic expression, and true power to the people since its very beginnings. Just for the record, this is not an experiment in limited self-government: it never was, but politicians love to say that because it means they can usurp the powers the Constitution legitimately gives to the people—not to them.

"Honor, justice, and humanity, forbid us tamely to surrender that freedom which we received from our gallant ancestors, and which our innocent posterity has a right to receive from us. We cannot endure the infamy and guilt of resigning succeeding generations to that wretchedness which inevitably awaits them if we basely entail hereditary bondage on them." Thomas Jefferson, Declaration of the Causes and Necessities of Taking Up Arms, July 6, 1775

What we have culturally is a pack of jackasses who believe they created everything they have from scratch. They created their infant nourishment, the schools they attended, the roads they were driven to the doctor's on, the library they used, the jobs they had before they started their careers, etc. This kind of cultural belief that you are not beholden to anyone, that you are a "self-made man," is what has ruined us throughout our existence as a free people. The so-called "rugged individualist" is a myth. Perhaps the freest non-Native Americans who ever lived were the early visitors to the great western lands of our realm who trapped and traded in the mountains of the west, the "Mountain men." Their lives are documented in legend, story, and song, but none of them, from the Bent brothers and Joe Walker to Jim Bridger actually made it all alone. They integrated into the various Native tribes, taking wives and fighting alongside the warriors for the betterment of the whole community. The ones who didn't do this aren't in the books and songs because they didn't survive long enough to make an impact. No one even knows they existed. There are no towns, cities, or places on our map pioneered by egotistical loners. The only way we settled the vast expanse of country that was to become America was by pulling together, working as one, and leaving the ego back wherever we came from. We faced obstacles that could not be overcome except by concerted collective effort—that is what made this country, and that is what sustains this country.

When Andrew Jackson left office, the reaction to his style of governance began to settle in. Jackson, who may still hold the title as the most treacherous person ever to hold the office, created an era of political chaos such as has never been duplicated (except during the Civil War and its aftermath) in American history. Jackson, who is the true founder of the modern Democratic Party, apparently never met a man or woman he couldn't betray. He was responsible for one of the most shameful and duplicitous regimes this nation has ever seen. Wholesale stealing of land from peaceful Native American tribes, the tortuous Trail of Tears for Cherokees, and the same for Shawnees came about from this type of rule. Those who supported Jackson forever dishonored our values and our trust. They replaced honor with greed, and even though I strive very conscientiously to avoid judgment on historical situations because I can't know the culture or the circumstance as well as those who lived it, this Jacksonian era is without doubt the start of everything that undermined our freedoms and our birthright. Gone was the idealism of Washington, Adams, Jefferson, Madison, and Monroe, and in its place greed took over. In the next twenty years the moves made by Congress and seven presidents would open the doors to corruption like never before, and the economy would evolve from one that was supposed to create opportunity and build equity for all into one that was leveraged and controlled by large financial institutions on Wall Street that were heavily backed by foreign interests. Every evil imaginable descended on the American citizen and anyone coming to our shores to find freedom—all brought to bear by their elected representatives. Nevertheless, the question of a republican form of government (a government by elected representatives) was not brought up then as it might be now because opportunity was always there for the citizen if he was willing to move to new territory.

Let's recap here. I have clearly shown that we who live in this great country have been nearly completely disenfranchised economically by the Wall Street crooks and our elected representatives who have taken an oath to uphold the Constitution and to represent their constituency, 80 percent of our people, i.e. the American Middle Class are living on just 15 percent of the wealth the nation produces. Their wages relative to inflation and their net worth have both decreased in the past twenty-five years at alarming rates no matter which political party held power. This inequity in the distribution of wealth has nothing to do with the national productivity, we are the most productive economy on Earth, yet we have pushed 51 million people into poverty. We have created an economy were every single middle class wage earner has seen his net buying power decrease and his net worth plummet. Worse, the opportunity he once imagined would be there for his children has vanished. He can no longer afford to send them to college; he cannot even hope that they will ever get a job, and he is certain they have gotten a third-world education.

Now I should have convinced even the most diehard member of either of our two political parties that the cause of this is the governance we have received from them. A frequent justification for the difference between our situation now and what the Founding Fathers established is that we simply live in different times, yet we've seen that our Founders were not some hayseeds who fell off the turnip truck, but brilliant people who saw the future and made provisions in the Constitution to allow for changes and for new and unexpected developments. Those amendments show clearly that the amendment process is viable and will work if you apply to it. We have not enacted any amendments in recent times because our politicians and their puppet masters do not feel the need to do so; they just ignore the Constitution and are assured of getting away with it because they have stacked the courts, including the Supreme Court, with their cronies, and they know that the carefully crafted system of checks and balances is completely out of kilter.

As for the Elite on Wall Street, the ones who take investment money intended to grow businesses and expand industrial capabilities while creating new jobs but instead throw it away on "debentures," firmly believe in and promote the myth of the self-made man. They want this myth in our schools, in our institutions, in our nightly news. Why, you ask? It allows them to hide the fact that they irresponsibly throw away your retirement funds and give themselves multi-million dollar bonuses for failures. The myth says they were entrepreneurs seeking legitimate advantage over their competitors. It doesn't allow them to be prosecuted for fraud, negligence, corruption, and deceit. Oh, and isn't it amazing that they never are prosecuted by our district attorneys? Let me see—who pays for their campaigns to get reelected? Was it the financial industry "contributions" that got them elected? Would that be a conflict of interest? Not in this country were the Elite make the laws.

Let's get back to that aberration given us by the European societies that some group in society is somehow better than the rest of society and should lead while the rest follow, i.e. the hierarchical social structure. This aristocratic view was widely held when we started this country back in 1776, which was precisely why we started a rebellion in the first place. Men born free did not see how someone claiming to be an aristocrat was better able to govern them than they were themselves. Very simple really, but somehow we have lost this feeling. Where are the protestors to the Patriot Act? Do we care so little for the Bill of Rights? Where are the protestors to the Wall Street bailout—why aren't they in the streets: oh yes, actually they are? Where are the protestors to the tax breaks the oil industry enjoys? Are we really brainwashed by the thinly veiled threats on their television and radio ads suggesting that any tax on their profits would mean higher prices for us? Of course the same Congress that would tax their over 100 billion dollars in profits for 2009 could also make it a crime to pass that tax on to consumers. Ever wonder why they don't do that? Remember we are talking about profits, not operating capital, profits that they will distribute to those few who hold preferred stock in their companies.

Now the Wall Street bailout is only the tip of the iceberg when it comes to the complete flip-flop of American values and distortion of American intentions. The incredible de-Americanization of our citizens created by our "public service" organizations; that is, public schools, state and local agencies, federal police forces, etc. has been nothing short of disheartening. Almost the entire structure and philosophy of these agencies created by our government to "serve the people" were put in place by the Democratic Party. Let it be understood that the concept of a national socialist state was never a belief of our Founders; it was not in their experience or in their thoughts, so why do we have a two-party system with one of those parties promoting a socialist welfare state? To be sure national socialism was the concept and philosophy of the Nazis. The reason this is so easily laid at the door of the Democratic Party is because it was deliberately promoted and pursued by its office holders since before the beginning of the twentieth century, though it started in earnest with Woodrow Wilson.

By any standard Woodrow Wilson was a geek academic who had not the slightest idea of how to lead a political movement, let alone a nation, and who foisted his constitutional revisionist ideas on everyone, despite having no practical background to understand the implications of what he was promoting. He managed to get us pulled into World War I, a war we had absolutely no vested interest in, he attempted to start the League of Nations, without first consulting the electorate on what they wanted, so he founded a international organization that his own country would not join, he promised progressive reforms like his Bull Moose Party opponent, Teddy Roosevelt, but failed to delivered most of them. Yet he is still hailed in our classrooms as a great president. Why? Because the teachers in those classroom were themselves never taught how to think independently. They were taught in a system that insisted that the Constitution was irrelevant and needed to be ignored. The interesting thing about our modern approach to the governance of this people is that it does not ever look back and critically evaluate a situation but insists on going forward with every failure and defending it to the last breath. Revisionism was promoted in the writings of several individuals within the academic community and later within the political rhetoric who wanted to "correct" the perceived shortcoming of the American Constitution. Of course, the academic community that most readily absorbed revisionism consisted of the Ivy League colleges of the northeastern part of our country. How can I say that? Because it is the graduates of these colleges that have presided over the dismantlement of respect for Constitutional government in the last 40 years. Count them on the Supreme Court, as our Presidents, etc. They routinely ignore the Constitution instead of changing it, because they were taught to do this in their Ivy League classrooms, especially in the law classrooms. If you don't believe, just attend one. So the question is not what made them accept revisionism, I have my own theory on that and present it here, but why do they now continue to undermine our most sacred institutions? It would surprise many contemporary readers to know that prior to this wholesale conversion to the revisionist philosophies, this group of colleges was known most for their adherence to both the letter and the spirit of the Constitution. Writers like Emerson and Thoreau celebrated the freedoms that America offered. Prior to this new revisionist thinking, the Constitution was looked on as an almost sacred document, the embodiment of all that it meant to be an American. And yes it was changed frequently; by the time of Wilson, we had nineteen amendments, and in the near century that followed we have had only seven, one of which was a reversal of a prior amendment on prohibition. So we have only six new amendments in over ninety years. What changed? What changed was the respect we had for the Constitution: if it is an irrelevant document, why change it? Just ignore it.

Well revisionism started with John Dewey and his doctrines of historic relativity and experimentalism, the alleged purpose of which was to use the education system to create social change. Then there was the movement associated with the writings of James Allen Smith and Charles Beard. Whereas Dewey wanted to educate the next generation to view their history as relativistic and to encourage them to engage in experimentalism with their Constitution; Smith and Beard hoped their movement would right the wrongs they saw in the social contracts that characterized the late 1870s and 1880s—the era of the robber barons. Actually these points of view were understandable given the excesses of the time. As in our own time, the wealthy elitists had bribed lawmakers and undermined the very structure of our government and our Constitution to fill their pockets with the nation's wealth and exclude any and all competition from sharing the wealth. History records the absolute corruption of the government at this time, just as it will eventually record corruption of the government in our time. It is interesting to see our government hounding other countries, including China, India, and Indonesia, on how it treats it's working class because in the late 1800s we had all of these same abuses: child labor, eighty hours (and sometimes more) in the work week, no hope of a wage increase despite inflation, unsafe working conditions—especially in mines—instantaneous firing if you complained, management lock-out to stop union activity. Both political parties always sided with the owners, not the workers, and called out the police and the National Guard to put down objections with violent force, killing hundreds in some cases.

Of course anyone then and now who opposes the will of Wall Street and the big corporations was shouted down as a "Communist," or a "Socialist" when all they were was a member of their local labor union. Interestingly people are still doing the same thing 150 years later, and some of us are still buying it even though we directly benefitted from the sacrifices of those labor union members. The odd thing about this revisionism is that it did not objectively look at the root causes of the corruption and inequality of the time and propose solutions based on a constitutional amendment: it decided that the Constitution itself was irrelevant and therefore should be discarded. But they knew this wouldn't fly with the American people, so they proposed doing this by reeducating the masses and by creating laws that simply did not fit into the constitutional structure, then securing lawyers, congressmen, and judges who would "freely interpret" the Constitution to bring about the changes they thought would cure the problems.

In academia there is a tendency to invent the new instead of doing the hard work to improve the tried and true. It seems it was lost on these "intellects" of the early twentieth century that the Constitution is more than a legal document; it is a covenant between the people and their government. Changing it requires rigorous pursuit of the amendment clauses prescribed in the Constitution, if only to ensure that all the people are aware of the changes being proposed and have the opportunity to weigh in on the decision. The revisionist movement was trying to avoid this process, and they succeeded brilliantly. Few citizens have any idea what the Constitution says, and fewer realize how much their government is operating in complete disregard of its provisions.

Of course, the buy-in of the academic community was ensured by using new terms that sounded so up-to-date and appealed to the sense of novelty and discovery. Einstein's relativity theory had made a big stir in the scientific and media circles, and even though few people actually understood it, it was good PR to seem to be in the know. Placing yourself squarely in the elite circles of academia meant absorbing these new terms into your own discipline. Academia thus responded to a social and political situation by inventing revisionism and undermining our most important tenet of governance—the constitutional covenant between the people and their government.

I have to make a distinction here for the sake of accuracy: There was a major political movement going on within the Republican Party in the time of Woodrow Wilson called the Progressive movement, which was not a part of the early revisionist movement and was headed by Theodore Roosevelt. It was successful in creating a great many social and economic reforms aimed at thwarting the robber barons. Both Woodrow Wilson and Theodore Roosevelt called their movements "progressive," but one was actually the antithesis of the other. The important distinction was that Roosevelt's progressivism had the people decide the issues and Wilson's progressivism had the government decide the issues and give them to the people. This is a major difference if you happen to believe that the people have as much, if not more, wisdom than the government or if you just happen to think that democracy works. Roosevelt was defeated in the election of 1912, when he left the Republican Party and created the Bull Moose Party. But under Theodore Roosevelt some of the most significant legislation ever created in this country was passed to begin to level the playing field. Roosevelt's reforms are still on the books today but have not been enforced since the 1960s. Certainly the Republican Party of today would not endorse a Teddy Roosevelt even for the position of dog catcher. I am amazed to this day that Americans, even Republicans, would choose to vote for Taft over Roosevelt. What were they thinking? Of course Wilson won, and the rest is history as they say. It might surprise some to know what the progressives under

Teddy Roosevelt wanted to accomplish. Here is their party platform:

- A national health service to include all existing government medical agencies

- Social insurance to provide for the elderly, the unemployed, and the disabled

- Limited injunctions in strikes

- A minimum wage law for women

- An eight hour workday

- A federal securities commission

- Farm relief

- Workers' compensation for work-related injuries

- An inheritance tax

- A constitutional amendment to allow a federal income tax

- The political reforms proposed included

- Women's suffrage

- Direct election of senators

- Primary elections for state and federal nominations

- The platform also urged states to adopt measures for "direct democracy," including

- The recall election (citizens may remove an elected official before the end of his term)

- The referendum (citizens may decide on a law by popular vote)

- The initiative (citizens may propose a law by petition and enact it by popular vote)

- Judicial recall (when a court declares a law unconstitutional, the citizens may override that ruling by popular vote)

However, the main theme of the platform was an attack on the domination of politics by business interests, which allegedly controlled both established parties. The platform asserted that "To destroy this invisible Government, to dissolve the unholy alliance between corrupt business and corrupt politics is the first task of the statesmanship of the day."

Some things never change. Let's hope that, if given the chance, twenty-first century voters will make better choices.

The current crop of Republicans says they are for limited government, free enterprise, and holding to traditional values. They support the Constitution and believe in all of its provisions. They think that whatever is good for business is good for America. They are conservatives. This is the prevailing problem: they wish to deregulate banking and insurance interests, distorting and destroying the very freedoms they say they are defending. This philosophy will bring us right back to the era of the robber barons.

The current crop of Democrats says we want unlimited government, regulated enterprise, and social consciousness. They will decide what is taught in our schools, and who we see as our doctor. They want complete social and economic control of our lives and will build vast bureaucracies to do it. They are liberals. This is exactly what Communists did to their populations.

Neither of these positions is democratic nor republican. Now the one thing left out of both statements, but the thing that has become overwhelmingly obvious to all American citizens since October 2008, is that both parties live and have their source on Wall Street. They bow to the financial god and will have no other gods before it. The only certain reality of American politics in the twenty-first century is the Political-Financial Complex.

If you are a Republican and you don't like the laws the Republicans are passing in Congress where do you go? Oh, that's right, we have a two-party system, you could go to the Democrats. Ah, but that doesn't work either because they are voting for the exact same elitist laws that the Republicans are voting for. It's too bad we don't have more political parties, isn't it? Or is it? Wouldn't that just create more ways for the Wall Street interests to deceive you as to who was really going to take up the cause of the American Middle Class?

My purpose in writing this is to bring us back together, and my belief is that so long as we have two political parties devoted to separating us, we can never achieve national unity. The picture painted by our schools is of two parties with their legions of followers fighting for the heart of America and alternately winning and losing elections based on the strength of their appeal to yet another legion of Americans who are Independents. Unfortunately, that picture is highly distorted and we all know it is; even the media knows it, though they will never admit it. In the course of this struggle, which now covers centuries, we have completely lost sight of the founding principles of our nation. No one in 1776 was saying they were conservatives, unless we count Tories (British sympathizers) as conservative. Certainly Ben Franklin, George Washington, and Thomas Jefferson did not think they were conservative. But equally certain they would never have embraced the revisionist liberalism of today.

What then was their intent and what kind of government were they trying to create? What drove them to risk everything they had, and everything they could ever hope to have, in outright revolution against a superior political and military power that almost certainly could defeat them? I suspect that many Americans, even those who consider themselves real patriots seldom, if ever, ask themselves this question. I would go further and say that most Americans have never had the question answered. I know this because I know the design and purpose of our education system: (1) produce students who have never learned how to think on their own and who have no skill at critical analysis, (2) eliminate all civics training and avoid any discussion of why we created this American system of governance, (3) always focus the students on their obligations to support the national agenda, be it war, economic competition, or influence spreading. If your experience of the education system was different from this, than it is likely you did not attend public school, and if you did, it is likely you attended it before 1960. The reason this is so certain is that both parties want our education system to function this way. Any real movement to return to the values that created this country is adverse to their interests—and certainly to the interests of Wall Street.

The one word that I suppose is listed in all the media editorial rooms in America as taboo is hypocrisy. Notice you will never hear it, even though it appears to be the guiding characteristic of our age, but then the news that is reported by the corporate media is more than just negligent—it is completely false. Let's examine just a few of the recent examples of this distorted coverage and ask ourselves what was going on behind the scenes. Frankly any logical answer eludes me. (1) The first Gulf War promoted and organized by George W. Bush (our fortieth president). He arranged for and financially supported a coalition of countries to fight a war on the other side of the globe against an enemy that we called our friend only a few weeks before. Certainly

27

that country, Iraq, had invaded Kuwait and threatened to invade Saudi Arabia. Now really, why do we care? I've heard the excuse that we were concerned for Israel. Maybe, but why? Saddam Hussein was one of the very few secular leaders in the Arab world; he was a ferocious enemy of Iran and had defeated them in battle, and he was the bane of the Muslim fundamentalists in all of Arabia. Yes, he was a ruthless and sadistic dictator, but so is Mugabe in Zimbabwe, Mubarak in Egypt, Kim in North Korea, Gadhafi in Libya, Assad in Syria, not to mention Amadinajhad in Iran. Actually there are dozens of ruthless and sadistic dictators in the world, and we do nothing. So why was it so necessary to do something this time? Who was really threatened? If you are buying the story that Israel was threatened, then I hate to break your illusions, but not even crazy Saddam was nuts enough to attack a country with nuclear weapons and think he would survive. Saddam was clearly focused on the oil revenue that is in the Persian Gulf and specifically Kuwait and Saudi Arabia's wealth. Why then would we want to protect them? Because they are our number one foreign supplier of oil? Why would Saddam take the Persian Gulf oil fields and then refuse to sell oil to his number one customer? That doesn't come close to the truth.

Were the Saudis our great friends? Well that depends on what you call a friend. If a friend is a Wahhabi Muslim fundamentalist who is using all the money you give him for his oil to build medrasases (fundamentalist Muslim schools) in Afghanistan and Pakistan that openly teach hatred for America and call us "The Great Satan" while encouraging, if not demanding, worldwide Jihad against us, then I guess they were our friend. But more likely it was because the Bush family owed the Saudis a great debt because they had bailed out George Junior when he spent $25 million dollars of family and investor money in west Texas wildcatting for oil that only turned up dry holes. Maybe because his father was vice president at the time, and likely to become president, they managed to find an area just off their coast in the Persian Gulf that he was allowed to lease and where he could make his fortune (Unger 2004). Do you still think that move was to cover our vital national interest? Wasn't it odd that when we had secured their freedom and continued to station troops there that one of their most prominent Wahhabi fundamentalists attacked our solders in their barracks and killed over 230 of them while the Saudi police protected him and let him escape? Of course I'm speaking of Osama bin Laden. Ever hear any of that on your nightly news?

Maybe all of that first Gulf War history had nothing to do with why we entered the second Gulf War and insisted that Saddam had weapons of mass destruction when the international inspectors said he didn't. Let's see…who was right about that? Funny thing about that second Gulf War: our president and vice president promoted it to the exclusion of the war against the people who did attack us, the Al Qaeda in Afghanistan. It could be argued that they even made certain the Saudi leaders of Al Qaeda escaped when we had them trapped early in the war at Bora Tura and our troops were told to withdraw without explanation. But then we did the same thing with Saudi citizens after 9/11 when, on presidential orders, all Saudi citizens in the United States were allowed to fly home even though the FBI wanted to talk with them about the attack and had established a no-fly policy for everyone else in the country. I'm certain that American citizens would not be allowed to fly away if the FBI wanted to talk with them. But after all, why would the FBI want to talk with them? Do you think it might have had something to do with the fact that fifteen of the nineteen attackers were Saudi? Could it be that this president and vice president were both oilmen and focused on

Iraq's oil and not our enemies? I guess that is why they felt it necessary to suspend the Bill of Rights in our Constitution and start "rendering" citizens and foreigners alike to places like Egypt, where our dictator friends could torture them. I wonder what old Ben Franklin would think about that. More especially, what would Madison, Jay, and Hamilton think about that after all the time and effort they devoted to seeing that a Bill of Rights was adopted, if only because the Constitution itself could not be adopted by the original thirteen states without it.

Of course our two political parties have started a tradition of suspending the very freedoms we are fighting for in times of war to make us safe. If you were a German American in World War I or World War II, you know what that is like, but even more grievous: if you were a Japanese American in World War II, you are familiar with American concentration camps arranged to keep you safe by none other than Franklin D. Roosevelt. You know it seems since the end of World War II, and even since the fall of the "Evil Empire," we have never been out of war. We are constantly fighting wars someplace in order to create democracies where they aren't wanted. This gives our politicians a constant excuse to suspend our constitution.

I think if you asked Ben Franklin, George Washington, or Thomas Jefferson why they fought the Revolution, they wouldn't say it was to be safe. If safe is that important to you, I suggest you move into a prison; those walls, that wire, and those guards will keep you safe. But maybe you won't have to move; just wait awhile, and our whole country will become a prison.

I don't know about you, but I always thought it was a bit hypocritical to say you are the party of conservative principles and be the first to create the Patriot Act, which certainly doesn't conserve our constitutional rights. Even stranger, this was done based on the fear of a man living in a compound in Pakistan, who supposedly has no means of communications except for Al Jazeera. Do you not think that is an odd excuse to suspend our Bill of Rights? I do. In World War II we were facing a legitimate threat to our freedoms and the freedoms of the whole world. The Nazis were a world-class military system with a keen determination to suppress freedom everywhere. They were undone by Russian, British, and American soldiers and British and American pilots. Do you see a threat like that existing now? So why is our Bill of Rights suspended, and why are we allowing ourselves to be frightened by the media and the government? What is the point of that? I do not think the promotion of a safe society is better than the promotion of a free society. I guess if I were a police state advocate I could see some use for that, but I just don't, probably because I'm an American.

Now back to my point: we have not been and we are not now being represented in any way by our two political parties. Neither party ever carries out what it says it will do on election day, nor does either party have any interest in keeping and holding our founding principles sacred. So why are we voting for them to represent us? Do the things I have listed really make you want to vote them into power? Not just national power, but power in every state of the union. If I still haven't convinced you that continuing the two-party system is not in your interest, then stay tuned: I've only just begun. But first a reminder for those citizens who belong to the Democratic and Republican parties, All over the world, but especially in the Middle East, people are rising up demanding their freedoms, willing to die, if necessary, to ensure their children live in liberty. Shame on you, you support and vote for ever more repressive regimes that can have only one outcome for your children—a police state. You are throwing away your heritage with both hands while people die to get only a little of what you have.

Here are some enduring statements that seem very timely made by the Father of Our Country.

"One of the expedients of party to acquire influence, within particular districts, is to misrepresent the opinions and aims of other districts. You cannot shield yourselves too much against the jealousies and heart-burnings, which spring from these misrepresentations; they tend to render alien to each other those, who ought to be bound together by fraternal affection." —George Washington, Farewell Address, September 19, 1799

"Much indeed to be regretted, party disputes are now carried to such a length, and truth is so enveloped in mist and false representation, that it is extremely difficult to know through what channel to seek it. This difficulty to one, who is of no party, and whose sole wish is to pursue with undeviating steps a path which would lead this country to respectability, wealth, and happiness, is exceedingly to be lamented. But such, for wise purposes, it is presumed, is the turbulence of human passions in party disputes, when victory more than truth is the palm contended for." —George Washington, Letter to Timothy Pickering, July 27, 1795

"There is but one straight course, and that is to seek truth and pursue it steadily." — George Washington, Letter to Edmund Randolph, July 31, 1795

HOW DO WE FIX THIS?

But now the question is raised here: Does a system of elected representatives still work as the best form of governance we can accomplish? Could we move away from representative government to pure democracy? If it's necessary, how would we do that?

Right now we have what is called a bicameral house of representative—two houses—an upper house called the

Senate and a lower house called the House of Representative. There is often strong disagreement between these two branches of our legislature. This disagreement acts to stifle most legislation and is used successfully by the career politicians to control the outcome of almost all legislation going through the Congress.

Only the most naive among us could not fail to recognize that the bicameral system works to lengthen the sessions of Congress and to create a constant excuse for doing nothing. It is expensive and it is a waste of time to maintain two houses, we only need one. It also creates special interest legislation that costs all of us. The idea that Congress could be in session for the entire year and still be unable to pass appropriations in time to stop a default on the government's operations was never a part of the thinking of the Founders. Travel was long and difficult in those days, and one did not take his family with him, yet being separated from your family for virtually the entire year was not acceptable. The reason for multiple representatives from the same state was to ensure a quorum of representatives so the Congress could get its work done. We all know the reason given for having two houses was to ensure that every state, even the smallest, had a say in the deliberations without having a disproportionate influence exercised by the larger states. But we are now over 300 million in population, and to say that any segment of population, based on geographic location, is represented in Congress is just ludicrous. The only geographic area represented in Congress is the island of Manhattan.

No one is represented by this system except the persons or entities wealthy enough to afford hiring lobbyists to meet with representatives and bribe (contribute) their way to getting what they want. Do we want to continue this ridiculous charade? It cannot be fixed by creating still more parties for the rich to bribe. It can only be fixed with a universal suffrage that allows all citizens to vote directly on the issues. This cannot be done while we continue to operate as though voting weren't important. When we vote, we need to have a national holiday—no exceptions given, except for emergency personnel, to any person or entities for not taking it. The adoption of these measures to ensure the voting process remains important means we ban (and enforce the ban) on the use of attack ads or any ad trying to influence the vote. It means that the remaining two senators from each state can recommend based on what is in that state's legitimate interests, not on what will help a crony. Like all political processes the focus of the participants can never be certain. If we remove the incentives to bribe and corrupt officials by taking the influence away from them, we can hope we have improved the system. But nothing is certain in politics.

Nothing like this will happen while we are still ruled by the Democratic and Republican parties. This kind of reform can only happen with a Constitutional Convention. Before that convention starts, we need the people of America to start working with their state representatives to change the laws concerning who may run in an election. Right now the two political parties are grandfathered in; they don't have to prove they have 15 percent, or 10 percent or 5 percent of the potential electors as all other parties do. Other parties also have to post excessive amounts of money to pay for the elections the Democrats and Republicans get for free. We have to change this now, or we just won't have any alternatives other than the two political parties, which is exactly what these election laws were designed to do for the two parties in power. We need more expression, not less, and we can never get it if we have no alternatives beyond the two parties we have now.

The idea of making it possible for more parties to enter an election may seem counter intuitive to the stated purpose of this book which is to eliminate the two-party system altogether. But it will be necessary, if we are to accomplish this goal in a peaceful way, to have an interim way to make changes until we can put those changes into the constitution. That will require electing political representatives who are committed to these reforms and who will then be able to control state legislatures and even the national government to gain the majority necessary to bring reform using the constitutional process. That majority is a full ¾ of the states if we really want to move these changes forward expeditiously.

Chapter 2
The Economy: Globalization and Multinational Corporations

There is a great truth to economics that the elitist (greedy) don't want you to know: all wealth, I mean all wealth, flows directly from you. It is your labor, your valuation, your interest in a commodity or product that makes it valuable. If that doesn't exist, then nothing is worth anything. When nothing is worth anything, the big corporate offices, the perks, the cars, the planes, the private island retreats all disappear. You are the one essential element without which nothing works. This is pure unadulterated truth.

Yet you are the one who gets price gouged by shifty bank practices when you take out a mortgage on a house, you get the hit when the oil companies feel like pumping up the profit picture to record highs, and you are the one who pays the high prices to the pharmaceutical companies when they need to cover executive salaries. You are also the one who is denied a job when the failures of the banking system cause economic collapse; you are the one who gets taxed to keep the Wall Street ball bouncing. You are the one who pays for the corporate wars to keep the supply side flowing. You are the one who shells out so congressmen can have lifelong security after just one term and receive exorbitant salaries and perks while they are in office. Yes, you are the least important element in the eyes of the Elite when it comes to economic justice, but nothing works without you. Isn't that ironic? You who fund the vast give away to corrupt third-world countries, you who give up your manufacturing job to the Chinese laborer so Wal-Mart and Costco can make bigger profits while the government gives multinational corporations tax incentives to take your job out of the country. And how do they sell this insanity to you? They tell you it is "globalization" and soon we will all be one big economy.

Just don't ask for a cost of living raise; don't expect to get your savings or your retirement if an Enron or a World Com gets into trouble. The trickle-down theory of economics was never actually espoused by any economist: it was made up by the Reganites to justify the enormous amounts of money they pumped to their cronies in the oil and financial sectors to "jump start" the economy of the early 1980s. I would be remiss if I didn't point out that it worked: Wall Street never saw such profits; the financial companies went on a binge that only ended when they went down with the Savings and Loan debacle and corruptions of the late 1980s. Remember them. But do you also remember that the average worker in America saw his paycheck flat line during those same years? Seems that trickle just never got down to them. Then, as now, the Elite make sure they are not impacted by their mistakes, they always have the American Middle Class to bail them out.

An excerpt from the *New York Times* (March 29, 2007) by David Cay Johnston shows that income inequality grew significantly in 2005 with the top 1 percent of Americans—those with incomes that year of more than $348,000—receiving their largest share of national income since 1928.

The top 10 percent, roughly those earning more than $100,000, also reached a level of income share not seen since before the Depression. This data is based on analysis of newly released tax information.

While total reported income in the United States increased almost 9 percent in 2005, the most recent year for which such data is available, average incomes for those in the bottom 90 percent dipped slightly compared with the year before, dropping $172, or 0.6 percent. The gains went entirely to the top 1 percent, whose incomes rose to an average of more than $1.1 million each, an increase of more than $139,000, or about 14 percent.

The new data also shows that the top 300,000 Americans collectively enjoyed almost as much income as the bottom 150 million Americans. Per person, the top group received 440 times as much as the average person in the bottom half, nearly doubling the gap from 1980. The disparities may be even greater for another reason. The Internal Revenue Service estimates that accurately taxes 99 percent of wage income but that it captures only about 70 percent of business and investment income, most of which flows to upper-income individuals, because not everybody accurately reports such figures.

Prof. Emmanuel Saez, the University of California, Berkeley, economist who analyzed the Internal Revenue Service data with Prof. Thomas Piketty of the Paris School of Economics said that in addition to rising incomes and reduced taxes, the equation should take into account cuts in fringe benefits to workers and in government services that middle class and poor Americans rely on more than the affluent. These include health care, child care, and education spending. The analysis by the two professors showed that the top 10 percent of Americans collected 48.5 percent of all reported income in 2005. That is an increase of more than 2 percentage points over the previous year and up from roughly 33 percent in the late 1970s. The peak for this group was 49.3 percent in 1928.

THE WEALTH DISTRIBUTION

In the United States, wealth is highly concentrated in a relatively few hands. As of 2007, the top 1 percent of households (the upper class) owned 34.6 percent of all privately held wealth, and the next 19 percent (the managerial, professional, and small business stratum) had 50.5 percent, which means that just 20 percent of the people owned a remarkable 85 percent, leaving only 15 percent of the wealth for the bottom 80 percent (wage and salary workers). In terms of financial wealth (total net worth minus the value of one's home), the top 1 percent of households had an even greater share: 42.7 percent. Table 1 and Figure 1 present further details drawn from the careful work of economist Edward N. Wolff at New York University (2010).

TABLE 1: Distribution of net worth and financial wealth in the United States, 1983-2007

	TOTAL NET WORTH		
	Top 1%	Next 19%	Bottom 80%
1983	33.8%	47.5%	18.7%
1989	37.4%	46.2%	16.5%
1992	37.2%	46.6%	16.2%
1995	38.5%	45.4%	16.1%
1998	38.1%	45.3%	16.6%
2001	33.4%	51.0%	15.6%
2004	34.3%	50.3%	15.3%
2007	34.6%	50.5%	15.0%

	FINANCIAL WEALTH		
	Top 1%	Next 19%	Bottom 80%
1983	42.9%	48.4%	8.7%
1989	46.9%	46.5%	6.6%
1992	45.6%	46.7%	7.7%
1995	47.2%	45.9%	7.0%
1998	47.3%	43.6%	9.1%
2001	39.7%	51.5%	8.7%
2004	42.2%	50.3%	7.5%
2007	42.7%	50.3%	7.0%

Total assets are defined as the sum of: (1) the gross value of owner-occupied housing; (2) other real estate owned by the household; (3) cash and demand deposits; (4) time and savings deposits, certificates of deposit, and money market accounts; (5) government bonds, corporate bonds, foreign bonds, and other financial securities; (6) the cash surrender value of life insurance plans; (7) the cash surrender value of pension plans, including IRAs, Keogh, and 401(k) plans; (8) corporate stock and mutual funds; (9) net equity in unincorporated businesses; and (10) equity in trust funds.

Total liabilities are the sum of: (1) mortgage debt; (2) consumer debt, including auto loans; and (3) other debt. From Wolff (2004, 2007, 2010).

In terms of types of financial wealth, the top 1 percent of households has 38.3 percent of all privately held stock, 60.6 percent of financial securities, and 62.4 percent of business equity. The top 10 percent has 80 percent to 90 percent of stocks, bonds, trust funds, and business equity, and over 75 percent of non-home real estate. Since financial wealth is what counts as far as the control of income-producing assets, we can say that just 10 percent of the people own the United States of America.

TABLE 2: Wealth distribution by type of asset, 2007

	INVESTMENT ASSETS		
	Top 1%	Next 9%	Bottom 90%
Business equity	62.4%	30.9%	6.7%
Financial securities	60.6%	37.9%	1.5%
Trusts	38.9%	40.5%	20.6%
Stocks and mutual funds	38.3%	42.9%	18.8%
Non-home real estate	28.3%	48.6%	23.1%
TOTAL investment assets	49.7%	38.1%	12.2%

TABLE 3: Wealth distribution by type other asset, 2007

	Top 1%	Next 9%	Bottom 90%
Deposits	20.2%	37.5%	42.3%
Pension accounts	14.4%	44.8%	40.8%
Life insurance	22.0%	32.9%	45.1%
Principal residence	9.4%	29.2%	61.5%
TOTAL other assets	12.0%	33.8%	54.2%
Debt	5.4%	21.3%	73.4%

The first thing to notice about these startling statistics is that they come from 2007, the latest year we have data for; of course, this data was before we experienced the Depression of 2008. Yes, I know the Elite want you to think it is just a recession, but that is just crap. Note in the New York Times article that the 2005 data is compared to 1928, the year before the Depression of the twentieth century; isn't it clear from this data that when wealth becomes so skewed in our economy we are likely to experience a collapse? The comparison and the subsequent collapse in October of 2008 are almost mystical. Of course it was October of 1929 when the twentieth century's Great Depression began.

In both depressions the driving element was that the disparity between rich and poor grew so large that the economy had no one to sell its output to. The rich had succeeded in so garnering the wealth of the nation that the poor had nothing left to buy with. In short their greed had actually killed the goose that laid the golden egg. We did, of course, manage to do this more than just twice in our republic's history, but these two stand out because the gap was so wide and the recovery so long.

Now a lot of those radio and television talk show hosts would like you to think that the 1 percent who own 34.6 percent of all privately held wealth got it the old-fashioned way by hard work and frugal living. They also want you to aspire to be like them and join their ranks by applying yourself to equally hard work and frugal living. By implication the other 19 percent who own 50.5 percent of the nation's wealth got it by hard work and frugal living, too. Let's be honest here many people who have obtained success in our capitalist system got that success by hard work and clearly focused objectives and they deserve to be successful. Many people who are not successful in our economy are not successful because they lost themselves in drugs, debauchery, and laziness. So what am I saying here? I'm saying we need to maintain our political and economic systems, but we need to go back to a level playing field for all. With the corruption introduced by the Political-Financial Complex we have seen the unbalancing of our systems in both politics and economics. The unbalancing has most effected small American businesses in favor of large foreign businesses and hard working, honest American Middle Class citizens in favor of rich financial gamblers who throw away the hard-earned money of the American Middle Class on debentures and anything else they can think of to con us with, and then get their corrupt political buddies to bail them out with wage earner taxes and the repeal of laws that would have made their actions illegal..

So we have a nation that is supposed to be democratic in which 85 percent of all privately held wealth is in the hands of just 20 percent of its citizens. This leaves just 15 percent of the nation's wealth for 80 percent of its people. Some of us live in the land of milk and honey, while most of us live in a third-world country. If you doubt the 80% are living in a Third World country then here are some more statistics that many finally get you to understand: More than 1 million US home owners have lost their homes since 2008 (Realty Trac); 50.7 million people in the US do not have health Insurance - 16.3% of the population (US Census Bureau); Officially 9.1% of the population is unemployed (US Bureau of Labor Statistics), that is 28 million people, but unofficially the number is more like 47 million people if you count those who have simply stopped looking; On a given night in February 2007, 842,000 (in 637,000 households) experienced homelessness – which translates to almost 10% of the population of people living in poverty. These statistics from the National Coalition for the Homeless are before the October 2008 meltdown. There are no newer figures available. The US Census Bureau reports that 48.7 million Americans are living in poverty as of 2009 the latest date the statistics are available. Do you think that is what our Founding Fathers had in mind?

You recall that in the preface we spoke of a nation of donkeys. One of the chief images of the donkey is that of one going down the road with a stick and a carrot. The carrot is tied to the stick and is held out in front of the donkey just far enough to keep him going toward it, but always too far ahead for him to actually get it. The donkey driver in this case is the radio and television talk show hosts, who belong to the top 20 percent, who constantly ply the notion that you can get the carrot. They love to deride anyone and everyone who suggests that the carrot is never going to be obtained. They spout the Elitist line that we live in a great country where everyone can obtain whatever carrot they want. The donkey's line up for this propaganda and keep running after the carrot and, more importantly, voting for the politicians who espouse the Elitist line. The worst thing anyone can do to these donkeys is to tell them that this just isn't so. What you have to understand here is that all of this talk show dribble is being paid for by the wealthiest 1%. They have a vested interest in keeping you misinformed. We realize that telling people their dreams are unattainable is a harsh and even cruel thing, and it isn't that we lack empathy for those who have dreams; however, it is necessary to tell the truth sometimes in order to bring people back to reality. Once you have firm footing in reality, you can make better decisions and move toward your goals in a more surefooted manner.

The truth here is that this country, this America, this revolution in human evolution, was hijacked a long time ago. Its promise, hopes, and aspirations, as expressed in the Declaration of Independence, were never realized:

We hold these truths to be self-evident, that all men are created equal, that they are endowed by their Creator with certain unalienable Rights, that among these are Life, Liberty and the pursuit of Happiness.—That to secure these rights, Governments are instituted among Men, deriving their just powers from the consent of the governed,— That whenever any Form of Government becomes destructive of these ends, it is the Right of the People to alter or to abolish it, and to institute new Government,

laying its foundation on such principles and organizing its powers in such form, as to them shall seem most likely to affect their Safety and Happiness. Prudence, indeed, will dictate that Governments long established should not be changed for light and transient causes; and accordingly all experience hath shewn, that mankind are more disposed to suffer, while evils are sufferable, than to right themselves by abolishing the forms to which they are accustomed. But when a long train of abuses and usurpations, pursuing invariably the same Object evinces a design to reduce them under absolute Despotism, it is their right, it is their duty, to throw off such Government, and to provide new Guards for their future security.—Such has been the patient sufferance of these Colonies; and such is now the necessity which constrains them to alter their former Systems of Government.

These maybe the most powerful words ever written in the name of freedom. Thomas Jefferson, Ben Franklin, and John Adams are without doubt the most determined revolutionaries this world has ever seen. Take another look at what these three brilliant men are saying. How long do you think they would live in a country that had 80 percent of its population disenfranchised by economic inequality before they took up the pen and the sword again? Isn't that what the revolution was all about in the first place? What does it mean to be free if you have no say in the economy, no say in the government, and no say in how your nation conducts itself in the world? I would suggest to you that those 20 percent who own this country, own it not by virtue of their hard work and frugal living, but by virtue of their ability to effectively lobby Congress for anything they want: special advantages in business, bailout money, laws that promote the exploitation of the masses (i.e. the middle class), no usury laws so they can gouge you on interest rates, constant escalation of utility rates, tax breaks to move your job to a foreign country, etc. There is no end to the advantages they have gained to exploit you and get every last dollar you have. They do it with 30,000 lobbyists on K Street in Washington, D.C. And it's all legal. What about this picture does not square with the words printed above?

SOME NOTES FROM THE BUREAU OF LABOR STATISTICS:

Manufacturing sector productivity grew 5.8 percent in the fourth quarter of 2010, as output rose 3.7 percent and hours worked declined 2.0 percent. From the fourth quarter of 2009 to the fourth quarter of 2010, manufacturing productivity increased 3.6 percent as output increased 6.4 percent and hours rose 2.7 percent (table A). Unit labor costs in manufacturing fell 2.9 percent in the fourth quarter of 2010 and decreased 3.0 percent from the same quarter a year ago (table A). Annual average productivity grew 6.0 percent from 2009 to 2010. Table C presents annual averages for the most recent five years. The nonfarm business sector experienced productivity growth of 3.6 percent from 2009 to 2010 and 3.5 percent from 2008 to 2009. However, the 2010 increase in output per hour was due to a 3.7 percent increase in output as hours edged up 0.1 percent, whereas the 2009 productivity gain resulted when output fell 3.8 percent and hours fell 7.0 percent. In both years, strong productivity growth in nonfarm business was accompanied by declines in unit labor costs. By contrast the previous three years (2006–2008) were marked by modest productivity gains and increases in unit labor costs of more than two percent.

In the manufacturing sector, productivity grew 6.0 percent in 2010, the largest annual increase in output per hour since 2003, when output per hour increased 6.3 percent.

The 2010 productivity gain reflected a 6.6 percent increase in output combined with a 0.6 percent increase in hours. Productivity grew 8.2 percent in durable goods manufacturing and 3.5 percent in nondurable goods industries (tables 4 and 5). Unit labor costs in the manufacturing sector fell 4.5 percent—the largest decline in annual manufacturing unit labor costs since the series began in 1988.

TABLE 4. Annual average changes in productivity and related measures, 2006–2010

SECTOR	NONFARM BUSINESS				
	2006	**2007**	**2008**	**2009**	**2010**
Productivity	0.9	1.6	1.0	3.5	3.6
Output	3.1	2.1	-1.1	-3.8	3.7
Hours	2.2	0.5	-2.1	-7.0	0.1
Hourly compensation	3.8	4.0	3.3	1.9	2.0
Real hourly compensation	0.5	1.1	-0.5	2.2	0.3
Unit labor costs	2.8	2.4	2.2	-1.6	-1.5
SECTOR	MANUFACTURING				
	2006	**2007**	**2008**	**2009**	**2010**
Productivity	0.8	4.2	-0.3	2.0	6.0
Output	1.5	2.4	-4.4	-10.8	6.6
Hours	0.8	-1.7	-4.0	-12.6	0.6
Hourly compensation	2.0	3.3	4.0	5.2	1.2
Real hourly compensation	-1.2	0.4	0.1	5.6	-0.5
Unit labor costs	1.2	-0.9	4.3	3.1	-4.5

A caution here, things expressed as percentages can be distorting and confusing. To do a real analysis you have to be able to compare that growth to other elements that represent similar measures of productivity. The corporate media is fond of promoting the productivity rate increases of the East Asian countries as outstanding and exceptional; by implication the American worker must be lazy. For instance China would report a productivity growth of 8.2 percent in 2010. So our increase of 6.0 percent is just not keeping up. Right? Not on your life. Americans are the hardest working laborers on the planet; we surpassed the Japanese in 1999. We work longer hours and we are more productive during those hours than anyone else. So why does the corporate media want us to think we just aren't keeping up? It could be they don't understand statistics, or it could be that their corporate bosses, part of that 20 percent, just want us to squeeze out another, even higher, productivity gain. All percentage figures used to reflect growth have to come from a base figure. So if you had a base figure of 12.00 as your units produced per laborer and the Chinese had a base figure of 6.00, and you increased your productivity by 6.0 percent while they increased their productivity by 8.2 percent, the Chinese now have a base of 6.49 and you have a base of 12.72. Your laborer is still doing almost twice as much as his laborer. The problem comes in when your laborer is making $15.00 an hour and his is making $2.50 an hour. Your laborer has to produce six times as much; two times as much won't cut it. The problem is not that American laborers are unproductive, as the corporate media would have you believe, but that we live in such a cost-inflated country. Note that China does not appear on the chart presented below, which is because they refuse to collect their data in the same way that all other countries do—to obscure the true productivity relationships.

TABLE 5. Manufacturing productivity, 2007–2008

In 2008, all economies experienced severe declines in annual productivity changes compared with trends over 2000–2008. Although the Republic of Korea and the United States led with productivity growth of 1.2 percent, these increases were much lower compared to 2000–2008 trends.

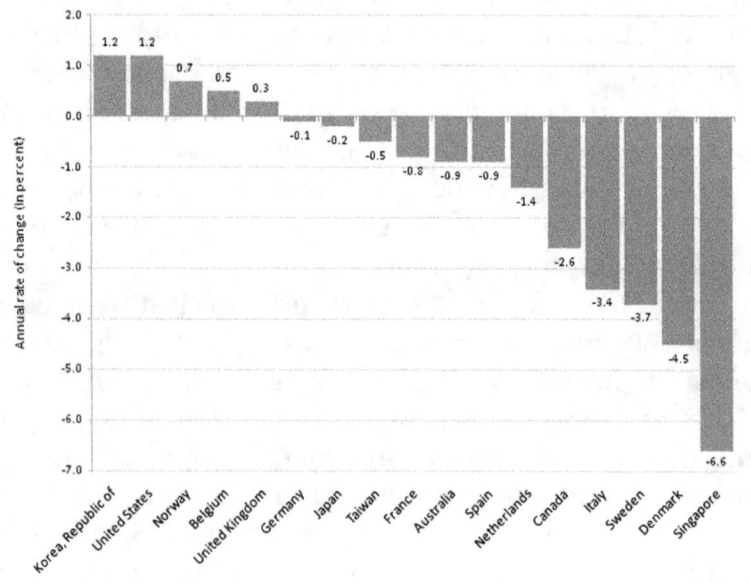

Source: International Comparisons of Manufacturing Productivity and Unit Labor Cost Trends, 2008.

So, let's see here: we know that the colonists were mad about the king's tax on tea, so they dressed up like Native Americans and threw the tea into the harbor. We know they conducted a boycott of English goods, we know they started hiking the prices of American goods sold to England. Do you think that economics might have been one of the causes of the American Revolution? I think we all know that the American Revolution was followed by the French Revolution. The French Revolution was a literal bloodbath for the French elite. You'd think people would learn that economic inequality is a certain harbinger of political change, but they never do. Not in France, not in Russia, not in Germany, not in Egypt or Libya, not anywhere. Greed, love of privilege, power, and elitism are the real drugs that will certainly take this country down, but we have no war on these drugs, at least not yet.

Our political parties want us to think that they are powerless to deal with the forces of globalization and multinational corporations. These are just changes to the world economy that they can't control. If you're buying that, I have some great swamp land in Florida I'd like to sell you. First of all, these changes came about because they pushed them through; yes, the Republicans and the Democrats pushed for this global economy because their sponsors on Wall Street wanted it. It didn't just materialize on its own—they made it happen. Why, you ask? Can you make more money selling your goods in one market or in twenty? Can you trash the planet twice as fast if you have access to all the world's resources and not just those of one country? Can you make bigger profits if your production costs are cut in half and your consumer market is kept at an arbitrarily high value so your products are much overpriced? Can you maintain your elite status as a member of the 20 percent club if you have only the stable and constant economy of a mature industrial nation?

Citizen, you have been sold out. The treachery of these two political parties makes anything that Machiavelli thought of look like Romper Room. Never have so many been sold into poverty by so few.

Let's say you are a congressman who's honest and really cares about your constituents, and you have a multinational corporate executive come to you and say, "If you don't give me a big tax reduction, I'm going to move my widget factory in Podunk, Ohio, to China." Are you helpless? Can you do anything but give in? What if you said, "Go right ahead and move your factory to China, but if you do, you will never sell another widget in this country for as long as you live." Now if you are the congressmen from the Podunk, Ohio, district you should be able to say that and know your party, even the opposition party, would support you. Problem is they won't. Your party will invent every excuse in the book to stop you from trying to make that threat stick. It doesn't matter which party you are from; they will not support you. It's not China who will object,—it's Wall Street. As we saw in October of 2008, political campaigns can stop in mid track, wars can go unfunded, but Wall Street cannot be denied. Do you have any delusions that this is not true? What is more, if you persist and even go public on stopping this blackmail, you will lose every position you have or will ever hope to have in the Congress—no chairmen of a committee for you—and when you run again for your seat, you will get nothing, nada, from your party for support. They will throw you away. This is why we have to get rid of the parties.

We guess we should explain ourselves here, lest the misinformation campaign have a feast on our bones. We are not trying to change our free enterprise form of economics. We 100 percent support free enterprise and hold strong opinions about other forms. Let's take Communism for example. Karl Marx and Friedrich Engels were two of the most unsuited people on the planet to be telling anyone how to run an economy, and the results prove my point. Marx was a super egotist who deeply resented his failures in both the academic and business world. Engels was the ne'er-do-well son of a wealthy aristocrat who never had to work a day in his life. Neither man had any claim to fame other than that they had written about and promoted this idea of Communism, "Das Capital." Their idea was to divide the population up into the bourgeois and the proletarians. The bourgeois were the wealthy professionals, the aristocrats, the bankers. The proletarians were actually everyone else, but in theory they were the working classes of an industrial society. They wanted the proletarians to rule, thus you needed a revolution. They got their revolution in exactly the countries they would never have thought would revolt, i.e. Russia and China. Why didn't they think these countries were ripe for their revolt? Because they believed that only countries like Britain, Germany, France, and the United States had real proletarian populations. You see Russia and China had largely agricultural populations at the time. Of course the ideals they promoted didn't work then, and would never work now, because people are not disposed to work their asses off and get nothing for it. Watching the goldbrick next to you do as little as possible while you work a full day and then going home with the same wage he gets is just not a formula for social or economic justice. As mentioned before, Marx and Engels just didn't get this because they had no background to understand work.

Of course we all know the economic system was a complete failure, and it produced only totalitarian regimes for a political system. But if you are one of those who think this might work, I suggest you move to North Korea. For much the same reason, the national socialist parties have failed as well: they provided a form of universal equality by taxing the most productive citizens down to the level of the least productive citizens. After watching this happen for a very long time in the Scandinavian countries, their governments started reforming their system to allow for more rewards to those who strived to do better. They only did this because they were rapidly slipping into a third-world economy. But the prime example of national socialism was Nazi Germany.

What they showed was this system wouldn't work unless you had some sort of overriding super class that rode rough-shod over all the lower classes. Then it works as an economic system, but not so much as a political system. There were some drawbacks even in the economic arena; you got your production on the backs of forced, slave camp labor that you did not pay and even forgot to feed. So naturally they had a very high attrition rate—due to death.

We think you get our point, we're not Communist or Socialist, but we are very sure we're not Democrat or Republican either. We like to think of ourselves as Americans.

If we take a look at what might have been the outcome of the American Revolution if it had not been subsequently hijacked by the greedy, we find a system that in no way resembles or imitates anything we have today. The Founders were from a largely agrarian society, and they found their source of livelihood in agrarian pursuits. Politicians, lawyers, academics, teachers, economists, and so forth have all used this fact as an excuse for why their ideas about economics would never work in a modern industrialized society, thus dismissing the idea that the Founders could have understood modern economics. Well that is very convenient if your goal is to justify an unworthy system, but if you really want to see if we have alternatives, you might not want to jump into that vat of hot oil so fast.

When the delegates to the Constitutional Convention met and began their deliberations, they saw an economy that was made up of farmers, merchants, tradesmen, and laborers. They had ship builders in New England cutting down the fine oak and pine of that region to produce trading vessels; they had farmers growing tobacco, corn, wheat, cotton, and barley, and selling it on the local and world market. They had foundry owners producing iron, carpenters making furniture, contractors building houses, transportation companies delivering goods, and potters making their wares.

Almost all of the investment capital that had built the country to this point came from the Old World, much of it from England. At this point we were no longer a colony and the English were not so sure about investing in a new country that might fail. For farmers to expand their fields, for merchants to offer more and better goods, for foundry owners to grow, they needed a source of capital. Someone had to be willing to invest in this country or we would stagnate. The question of creating a central bank arose, and it was a divisive issue: the delegates from New York, led by Alexander Hamilton, wanted it; other delegates from more rural areas, didn't. Hamilton forged some very smart alliances with sources in the Caribbean and Europe, and with the landed aristocracy of the Hudson River Valley in New York to bring in capital. He became George Washington's chief of the treasury. He was very good at it, but his actions and his ambitions were not without opposition, so he became a kind of martyr to the new economic system when Aryan Burr shot him dead in a duel.

A major problem facing the first federal government was how to deal with the financial chaos created by the American Revolution. States had huge war debts, and there was runaway inflation. Almost all aspects of the economy looked dismal throughout the 1780s. Economic hard times were a major factor in creating the sense of crisis that produced the stronger central government under the new Constitution.

In the immediate post-colonial period, one of the first issues of contention concerned industrialization, or the respective roles of agriculture and manufacturing, and the parallel debate over the division of economic powers between states and the federal government. These disagreements expressed themselves in the political division between Republicans and Federalists. The individuals representing the extremes of this argument were Thomas Jefferson and George Logan on the side of agriculture and republicanism, and Alexander Hamilton on the side of industrialization and federalism.

The first issue that Hamilton tackled as Washington's secretary of the treasury concerned the problem of public credit. Governments at all levels had taken on so much debt during the Revolution, and the commitment to paying them back was not taken very seriously. By the late 1780s, the value of such public securities had plunged to a small fraction of their face value. In other words, state IOU's—the money borrowed to finance the Revolution—were viewed as nearly worthless. Hamilton issued a bold proposal to resolve this. The federal government should pay off all Confederation (state) debts at full value. Such an action would dramatically enhance the legitimacy of the new central government. To raise money to pay off the debts, Hamilton would issue new securities (bonds). Investors who had purchased these public securities could make enormous profits when the time came for the United States to pay off these new debts.

Hamilton's vision for reshaping the American economy included a federal charter for a national financial institution. He proposed a Bank of the United States. Modeled along the lines of the Bank of England, a central bank would help make the new nation's economy solid through a more stable paper currency. This concept of a central bank faced significant opposition. Many feared it would fall under the influence of wealthy, urban northeasterners and speculators from overseas. In the end, with the support of George Washington, the bank was chartered with its first headquarters in Philadelphia.

The third major area of Hamilton's economic plan aimed to make American manufacturers self-sufficient. The American economy had traditionally rested upon large-scale agricultural exports to pay for the import of British manufactured goods. Hamilton rightly thought that this dependence on expensive foreign goods limited the American economy, especially when compared to the rapid growth of early industrialization in Great Britain. Rather than accept this condition, Hamilton wanted the United States to adopt a mercantilist economic policy. This would protect American manufacturers through direct government subsidies (handouts to business) and tariffs (taxes on imported goods). This protectionist policy would help fledgling American producers to compete with inexpensive European imports.

Hamilton possessed a remarkably acute economic vision. His aggressive support for manufacturing, banks, and strong public credit all became central aspects of the modern capitalist economy that would develop in the United States in the century after his death. Nevertheless, his policies were deeply controversial in their day. Many Americans neither liked Hamilton's elitist attitude nor his commitment to a British model of economic development. His pro-British foreign policy was potentially explosive in the wake of the Revolution. Hamilton favored an even stronger central government than the Constitution had created and often linked democratic impulses with potential anarchy. Finally, because the beneficiaries of his innovative economic policies were concentrated in the northeast, they threatened to stimulate divisive geographic differences in the new nation.

Nevertheless, Hamilton's economic philosophies became touchstones of the modern American capitalist economy. Hamilton had turned the tables on his opposition. Where Jefferson, Madison, and Randolph argued that the federal government had no power to incorporate a bank because it was not explicitly allowed to do so in the Constitution, Hamilton retorted that the government enjoyed all powers necessary to its functioning that were not explicitly forbidden. Hamilton's logic was unanswerable. From that day forth the doctrine of "implied powers" increasingly dominated legal interpretation of the Constitution. Hamilton had gained not one but two victories, the establishment of the Bank and the widespread acceptance of the doctrine of implied powers.

Washington signed the bill on February 25, 1791, and the centerpiece of Hamilton's creation was a strong federal government. However, the triumvirate of Madison, Randolph, and Jefferson was horrified that their fellow Virginian, George Washington, had signed the bill. The agrarian trio would not soon forget.

Quite likely, Washington signed the Bank into law because he knew that the financial system was as yet incomplete and that the country needed a national bank, both to aid the government's fiscal operations and to help unify the nation's credit and capital markets. Detractors believed the bank was so colossal that it was capable of many evils. They labeled the Bank a monopolistic monster that would corrupt the entire society. Why was this fear so strong? In the twenty-first century, when over ten thousand banks of various sorts exist in America, it may be difficult to comprehend the hostility, but in the 1790s, banks, and in particular a bank with a unique national charter (charters were usually granted by states), were looked upon with profound suspicion. The anti-bank advocates were terrified that the Bank could usurp power. After all, was the Bank not going to be guardian of the public money? And if that was the case, was that not too great a temptation for mere mortals? The entire Constitution was based on checks and balances, but was private ownership enough of a check on the Bank? Detractors also labeled the Bank as an enemy of farmers— at a time when some 90 percent of the population toiled in the fields and barns.

Southerners especially feared the institution. Many thought it would drain the economy of gold and silver. Others who did not understand that banks had to redeem their notes and deposits for specie on demand feared the onset of rampant inflation once its presses commenced printing. Southern delegates also opposed the Bank's two-decade lifespan. (Unlike today, all early U.S. corporate charters were of finite duration.) Commenting on the proposed length of the charter, Madison was purported to have said that "twenty years was to this country as a period of a century is to the history of other countries—there was no calculating for the events which might take place." Southerners also feared that the Bank, which was head-quartered in Philadelphia, would be used as an excuse to renege on the deal struck to move the seat of government to the Potomac in 1800.

On one level, Hamilton had difficulty comprehending the agrarian critique. Unlike many of his contemporaries, Hamilton did not see the issue of state versus federal power as a zero-sum game. He was, after all, one of the leading proponents of federalism (note the small f), the notion that the states and the national government could share power. The creation of the Bank of the United States, for instance, did not preclude the formation of state banks and in fact ultimately made life for state banks easier. The assumption of state debts did not preclude borrowing by state governments in the future and in fact made it easier for states to borrow again. Perhaps most importantly, the different levels of government served to check and balance each other. Hamilton's perception of power as something other than a finite sum was decades ahead of its time. However, the antagonism went much deeper than the issues. Agrarians thought Hamilton a tyrant who had designs on ruling the new country himself. In their opinion, he had duped Washington. Ironically, though, while many Republicans distrusted Hamilton, they not only did not destroy the financial system and in many cases strengthened it.

Thanks to Hamilton, the nation's credit was so good that it easily borrowed to purchase Louisiana and to fight the War of 1812. The first Bank helped to keep the macroeconomy on an even keel by checking the note issue of state banks. The entire nation had a single unit of account, the U.S. dollar, which was firmly defined in terms of gold and silver. Fire and marine insurance was almost fully formed; life insurance lay just over the horizon, as did trust companies, savings banks, and building-and-loans. Great leaps in manufacturing—ultimately funded by banks and capital markets—began just a few years after Hamilton's death. Most importantly, economic growth—increases in real per capita output—was picking up steam, soon literally as well as figuratively.

Distrust of the Bank nevertheless continued, and the issue did not go away even though the early 1800s would see three Virginians in a row as president of the United States. Dissent continued through Andrew Jackson's time, when he vetoed it yet again and finally sunk the Bank for good. By then securities markets, state banks, and even insurance companies had developed and grown up under its protections and were able to continue without it.

So it was Hamilton's vision to create and perpetuate our economic policies that prevailed and made the system we have today. Was he an elitist? No doubt. Was his system designed to create economic inequality? No. Despite opposition from Madison, Jefferson, and Reynolds in particular, he was not intentionally trying to create a system of leveraged privilege for the wealthy. That would come later. Hamilton was, in short, the creator of the U.S. financial system, the engine of America's remarkable nineteenth-century economic and political transformations. From Financial Founding Fathers: The Men Who Made America Rich (Wright 2006).

How do we fix this?

In the first chapter we addressed the political parties and how they have undermined the Constitution and the American middle class. In this chapter we need to address how to fix one of the greatest wealth inequities that has ever existed in the history of our country. The Democrats will tell you that it can be fixed by taxing the rich at a higher rate than the poor. The Republicans will tell you that if you just stop taxing the rich they will jump-start the economy and the resulting prosperity will somehow trickle down to the middle class. If you are still buying either of these arguments, you were born yesterday.

The fix to a problem of this magnitude is not going to come from government; inequality is too profoundly entrenched in our lives for government to ever be able to solve it. We hope you will recall how we started this chapter; we told you the great truth about money matters- nothing has value unless you say it has value. If the Democrats tax the rich, will any of that money ever get to the middle class as an increase in earnings or as a boost in net worth? It will go to the government, not you; it will pay for ever more fancy embassies and more wars and a lot more perks for your favorite representative. You and your children will never see a dime of it. Be sure it won't even pay down our tremendous indebtedness that will stifle your children and grandchildren with taxes and lessened opportunities. If the Republicans get to cut taxes on the rich and provide absolutely no regulations on the financial institutions, will you ever see a dime of that money? Do I have to tell you that the money will go for ever bigger bonuses on Wall Street, will fund the gamblers who throw away your money on debentures while failing to invest in our industry and our infrastructure? Do you not know that the tycoons of industry will line their pockets by buying more private island resorts, airplanes, and yachts? Are you naive enough to think they will spend their new wealth on increasing wages and improving working conditions?

No, we need a fundamental change in our economic system to distribute the wealth of this nation in some equitable way. That change involves truly revolutionary measures and would never be allowed by our present government representatives. Do you not know that whoever controls the purse strings gets to call the shots? In the prior discussions we hope we were able to show you that it is the American Middle Class who is the most targeted prey animal on this planet. Absolutely everybody wants a shot at you, as part of the middle class. The politicians want to find ever more ways of prying money out of you so they can maintain their power and influence. The gangs on Wall Street want to be allowed to charge you whatever fee or interest rate they can think of so they can live like kings and buy their congressmen. The captains of industry want at your wallet so they can sell you useless and dangerous drugs, gasoline at exorbitant prices, automobiles that fall apart before you can get them paid for, and airline tickets that cost twice as much as advertised while you are treated as though you were entering Dachau when you try to board.

In the original concept of our democratic society the Founders believed that societal grievances, such as these, would be addressed through the representatives who were sent to Congress. The idea that they would be organized into parties came after the Constitution was written. The model of a society that functioned in a just and equitable way was quickly hijacked by a model of special interest, greed, privilege, and ambition. This wasn't arrested by the elected representatives—it was abetted by them. In retrospect it was inevitable that man, at this stage of evolution, was not up to the lofty goals and utopian visions of our Founders.

Now we have an economic and political system that is supposed to handle citizens' grievances and provide leadership yet has no interest in hearing their grievances, or making any changes that would benefit their constituency. So how do we find the leadership to change our economic lives and to provide real representation for the American middle class? To get a piece of our intended inheritance we have to change our political paradigms. We live in a democracy where the middle class is not represented, yet the middle class is still, by far, the largest group of citizens in that democracy. This lack of representation has led to a tremendous economic disenfranchisement and a completely inequitable political balance of power. The middle class should have the control in this democracy, but they have no better standing than did serfs and peasants in the Middle Ages of European history.

So long as you vote for either of the two political parties, this situation will remain, and it won't just impact your life: it will have your children and grandchildren growing up in a serf society that allows them no advantages in life. The stakes are very high. They will remain the prey you have become with no job security, no access to college, no way to stop constantly escalating costs of just living, no possibility of seeing significant wage increases, no relief from bloated government, no allowance for individual freedom in the ever increasing police state atmosphere, and no change in sight in the future.

The new paradigm requires you to stop voting, to hit the streets like Martin Luther King taught us to do in non-violent protest of the theft of the nation's wealth by the few and the greedy. You must demand that the Wall Street bankers be stopped, the New York Stock Exchange and the Chicago Board of Trade be closed down permanently; that investment be spent on growing businesses, not on making individuals wealthy at the expense of the nation; that pharmaceutical companies stop using American citizens as guinea pigs; that ostentatious overseas spending on embassies, dictators, military bases, and oil kings be stopped; that Congress make all of its laws apply to its own members, including the requirement to pay into Social Security and a health care plan they pay for out of their pockets, not ours; that the buildup of unprecedented police forces be stopped and rolled back to reasonable levels; that all wars on the anthropomorphized enemy of the day be stopped— they produce no results and they waste money; and that Congress roll back their crooked pay increases to where they were in 1970.

"A rigid economy of the public contributions and absolute interdiction of all useless expenses will go far towards keeping the government honest and unoppressive." —Thomas Jefferson, letter to Lafayette, 1823

But you say they won't listen, and you are right—they won't until you do the other thing that will make them listen. You refuse to buy anything until they do. That's right—you put on the worst economic boycott the world has ever seen. You stop paying into 401Ks, you stop buying life, health, and auto insurance. You drive as little as possible, you make only life-sustaining purchases, and you slow the economic engine to a crawl. You are then hitting them where it hurts. Until you do this, they will not stop treating you like a serf.

Remember nothing has value unless you give it value. This boycott will say that nothing has value until the government starts giving you the inheritance the Founding Fathers intended for you. It is your birthright and it belongs to you. Nonviolent protest, economic boycott, and some real old-fashioned frugality will get you that birthright, but all of the American middle class must be willing to do this until we get back our freedoms. This needs to be organized at the grass roots level, not by national or even state alliances, but at the town and city level. Nothing less will work.

Chapter 3
The Media: Corporate Control of What You Hear and See

"**Liberty cannot be preserved without a general knowledge among the people, who have a right, from the frame of their nature, to knowledge, as their great Creator, who does nothing in vain, has given them understandings, and a desire to know; but besides this, they have a right, an indisputable, unalienable, indefeasible, divine right to that most dreaded and envied kind of knowledge, I mean, of the characters and conduct of their rulers.**" —John Adams, "A Dissertation on the Canon and Feudal Law," 1765

Most Americans like to come home in the evening and unwind after a hard day by catching up on the latest things happening in their world. They tune into the national TV broadcast networks to find out what disasters have befallen the world and what improvements have been made. Few, if any, realize that they are watching a highly managed piece of information tailored to tell them only what the corporate world wants them to know. Now if you point this out to many American they will immediately deny it. Preferring to believe that we have a free press, as within our Constitutional rights (First Amendment). But here is an area that certainly requires that wise counsel of Thomas Jefferson when he said, **"The price of liberty is eternal vigilance."**

What you are actually getting is a very meticulously scrubbed version of the day's events that is designed to make you believe that the world is a very dangerous place and your only hope of survival is to push for more police power and more government control. Any good news is confined to simple-minded exploitive pieces at the end of the news segment that tell you nothing about your world, your nation, or your community, but show you some guy in Iowa who grows 1,000-pound pumpkins. He gets his three minutes of fame and you leave the news segment in a state of mental numbness.

You have to follow the money. Those sparkling personalities you see every night pitching you the bad and the very bad with a smile are nothing more than puppets. If you need proof, let's take a quiz and see what our news media has given us for answers: Don't worry: if you can't answer the questions from forty years ago because you were too young, you will not be graded on that portion of the test.

Let's start with a basic: Why did Osama bin Laden and his mostly Saudi Arabian followers (fifteen of nineteen were Saudis) attack the US?

(1) Because the United States put soldiers on Saudi soil to defend them from Saddam Hussein?

(2) Because he wanted to destabilize the world markets and ruin the Saudi government so he could take over?

(3) Because he wanted to attack the country that supported Israel?

If you regularly view the evening news, you might have been tempted by answers one or two. I don't know if you can trust anything bin Laden says because he is, after all, a very devious guy, but all of his own propaganda says he did it to get revenge on the West, America in particular, for imposing Israel on a Muslim country (Palestine). I think if we are going to go to war and commit our young people to die to protect us, we should at least know what the war is all about, don't you? Now don't mistake my meaning or intent here: I do think we have no choice but to fight Osama and his murderers who claim they murder in the name of Islam. I do believe the world will know no peace until they are all in the graves they so wantonly covet. I would personally be very happy to aid them in that quest. But I would like to know the truth when I go to war, not some fabrication of the politicians and the media.

We Americans have a long history of fabrications when it comes to war, and it shows no sign of stopping. We vilified the native races as an excuse to attack them and take their land; we took advantage of the explosion of a boiler on an American ship docked in Havana harbor to attack the Spanish and take Cuba for our own. That was followed with an attack on the Philippines to do the same thing. So fabrication, out-and-out lying, is not new to our people or our nation. I think we all know about the media hype leading up to the Vietnam War. If you don't, go back and pick up a magazine from the early 1960s in your library, though you could as easily pick up a media clip from the era, or whatever. The corporate world wanted us to go to war to get the economy jumped-started, and Vietnam looked like a good way to do that. By the way, the media likes to go back to that time, pretending those were the days of Camelot, and the one thing they like use is President Kennedy's inaugural speech, "Ask not what your country can do for you, but what you can do for your country." If that isn't a preparatory speech to get a war started, I would like to know what is.

Now another quiz. If you are old enough, you will find this interesting, but if you're not old enough, I think you will still find it informative. Was Vietnam the only country in Southeast Asia the United States invaded during the Vietnam War? I think most of you will say no; you will acknowledge that we invaded Cambodia. But that is where the waters get a little murky. What actually happened as a result of our invasion of Cambodia, and why? Hint: "the killing fields."

Now here is a history lesson that the news media did not give. We moved into the neutral country of Laos as "advisors" to assist the Royal Laotian Kingdom in its own defense. To do that we sent American airmen, known then as Air Commandos, to teach the Lao, who were Buddhists pacifist, to defend themselves. These men, not Air America, like the Hollywood version would have you believe, fought the Pathet Lao, a North Vietnam front organization made up of mostly Thai Chin tribesmen, to a resounding defeat. At the same time, they became so successful in their missions over the Ho Chi Minh Trail that they literally shut down the Mu Gi Pass and forced the enemy to go through the swamps of the Demilitarized Zone to supply the South. Bet you never read anything like that in your history books or in your newspaper. But to really understand this you need to know more.

These American and Royal Laotian units were located about 20 miles outside of the capital city of Vientiane in a place called "Camp Friendship." Because Laos was a neutral country and was supposed to be left untouched by both sides according to a Geneva Peace Agreement between the world powers, the U.S. State Department, who had a much bigger hand in running this war then most now understand, had to pretend it didn't exist. So they would not allow the airmen stationed there to come into the town. That way they could maintain their innocence about the American military presence in a neutral country. That certainly put the airmen assigned there in a peculiar position. They had to dress as civilians, for one thing, but it did not stop them from becoming one of the most effective counter-terrorism units that ever fought under the American flag, the exaggerated stories of the Air America mercenaries notwithstanding.

I think it should be pointed out that these airmen were under orders from the then head of the Defense Department to not even go out in search of downed American flyers in Laos; I'm speaking, of course, about McNamara, the infamous secretary of defense under the Johnson administration. It should also be pointed out that this was the order in later years because the State Department, under Henry Kissinger, didn't want to have any international incidents of Americans being caught fighting in a neutral country. Now I didn't say these orders were followed by the Air Commandos; I just said they were passed down by the two above mentioned politicians. Did I mention that these airmen were asked to teach the pacifist Lao how to fly their T-28 prop plane trainers, the same trainers used in WWII? Did I mention that the successes of these units were paid with a very dear price, some units seeing 87 percent casualties? Or that units stationed in Thailand were flying daily missions into Laos and South Vietnam in unarmed Piper Cubs (Bird Dogs) to spot the enemy troop and materials movements on the Ho Chi Min Trail and that these planes could actually be shot down with a pistol? Keep in mind my earlier statement about their successes and now realize how terribly hard that was.

There is a greater lesson here that has direct application to today's wars, which is why I am pursuing this. The success of these airmen came because they had a very effective support team, and I'm not talking about military logistics—they had almost none of that. Starting in the 1950s America had sent the country of Laos U.S. aid. This aid came in the form of supplies, but more importantly it came in the form of Americans who could actually do things: doctors, farmers, and construction workers, among others. In Laos, as in almost all other countries, these Americans made a tremendous impression on the local population. They built roads, supplied safe drinking water, built clinics and schools. They achieved way beyond their means because they were dedicated and hard-working—exactly what Americans have always been in building community. That background gave those Air Commandos a trusting population that had their back. The Americans were proactive; they went into the hills and stayed with the Hmong, the Khmers, the Meo, and the Laos. They trained them to protect themselves from the terrorist Pathet Lao, who loved to attack a village at midnight, round up all the elders and knee-cap them, steal or destroy all their food provisions, and leave the village to struggle with starvation and caring for the wounded, a most effective way of neutralizing them. Never mind that these villagers had never done anything to assist in the war one way or another. That didn't matter to the North Vietnamese who masterminded these atrocities. It was all part of a plan of systematic terrorism. I wish Americans would keep this in mind while the politicians try to "win over" the North Vietnamese government. Why? So the multinational corporations, who run our country, can profitably exploit their large and educated labor force, send your jobs there, and increase their profits—that's why.

Lest you think I'm going to insist we live in the past, I have to say I think we must engage all the people on this planet, but it is our intent and motive that I believe we need to clean up before we start creating future enemies; we have plenty of those to last us many generations.

During the Vietnam War, the grunts—foot soldiers on the ground—really didn't have any voice. They were not interviewed as they are now, and they were not asked any-thing by reporters. One reason for that had to do with loca-tion; the soldiers were in the field, and the reporters were in a bar somewhere. But the other had to do with biases; the media thought the soldier was there to do what he was told and really had no say, so why ask him? Besides it didn't play well with the network executives if he had something negative say; that wasn't what they wanted presented on prime time TV back home.

Now when I was in ROTC and we talked about war tac-tics, we were instructed that the United States would not fight an Asian land war with conventional weapons because it was not winnable. The illustration given was that you could sit there shooting your machine gun and killing the enemy every second of every minute of every hour of every day for a year without making a dent in the population because it was increasing faster than you could kill them—actually quite true. But what was important to an overpopu-lated country was land. Control the land, deny the enemy the use of that land, and you would win the war—also quite true.

So we enter a war in Asia, even as I was learning these lessons, and the first thing we do is to resolve not to use unconventional weapons, i.e. nukes. Then on the battlefield we adopt the tactic of taking an enemy position, a hill, a for-ested area, a village, and then turning around and leaving it. We didn't secure it from his use; we just gave it back. Now how could that be? Didn't the military read their own teach-ing materials? Could it be that politicians, not military men, were calling the shots? The media liked to tell us we got into the Vietnam War, which I admit was certainly not called for by any stretch of the imagination, because the military wanted to go in there as a strategic move to stop the fall of the entire region to the Communist forces. I know that was the party line (of both parties), but was that really why we went into Vietnam? Supposedly we believed a domino effect would occur if one Southeast nation fell, and we would lose all of Asia. We also had this theory of the "rim land" to contain communism by surrounding the Communist nations to prevent their expansion. Hind sight proves both of these theories wrong, but let's look at the logic of these reasons with as little reliance on hindsight as possible.

In that same ROTC class Captain Curran, already a Vietnam veteran in 1962, was teaching us the basic sources of military success. I remember hearing "Mass at the critical point," "There is no benefit from prolonged warfare," "All warfare is based on deception," and "Take the advantages of interior lines." Oh, wait a minute, what does that last one mean? Is there an advantage of having interior lines? I think so. Let's say you are a country surrounded on all sides by hostile forces; your forces and the enemy forces are roughly equal, but the enemy has to supply his forces across the entire perimeter of your border from the outside, the circumference. That means he has to have large and very long logistical lines of supply that are often exposed to your attack, whereas you have the advantage of supply lines that are entirely within the territory you control and are therefore not easily attacked—really a simple and readily understood principle. Given that the Communist world in 1962 was exactly the model for this principle and we were the ones who would have the perimeter if we developed "rim land" theory policy, why on Earth would we do so? Unless of course, it wasn't a military policy, but a political one.

If it is not logical that the military would have desired the "rim land" for strategy, and anyone who knew military tactics would know this, then what was our real objective in Vietnam? I really doubt it was a military objective. So as not to foster even more conspiracy theories I will let you answer

that question, but I will point out that the most promul-
gated red herring of our time is the "Military-Industrial
Complex. The media loves to talk about this and to point
fingers and rail against this, all the while ignoring the Political-Financial Complex that is robbing us blind. I should
also point out that while Washington is indeed ringed by
many companies trying to get government contracts, the
so-called "beltway bandits," as a rule of thumb these aerospace companies usually see about a 4–6 percent margin
on their business, not any better than wholesale. Try telling
a Wall Street banker that we are going to hold his margins
to 4–6 percent; I think you know Congress would have to
hold special sessions to stop that. Try telling those bankers
we are going to stop their pilfering of the investments sent
to them to grow American industry by limiting their annual
compensation and we would have financial meltdown. Our
two political parties would have apoplexy.

Now in recent years, since the first Gulf War, the military has extended the opportunity to send reporters with
units and to allow those reporters access to even the lowest ranked among the troops. This is a wise policy because
the accuracy and the reality of combat have been measur-
ably improved, and the opportunity to misrepresent has
lessened. We no longer have radio and TV talk shows suggesting we are at war because the troops wanted it that
way, as actually happened in the Vietnam conflict, and
we no longer have reporters espousing that the troops
are all murderers straight from our prisons, who came to
the conflict to kill people legally. Now when they return
from battle, the head of the Veterans of Foreign Affairs
(VFW) doesn't call them crybabies because he thinks
they shouldn't complain about fighting a war that has
them walking away from military objectives, handing
them back to the enemy. The media and their sponsors

know that could not be maintained today. The improvement has reached every area of military life; the Veterans Administration has been asked to actually be responsive, the returning soldiers are getting some post-traumatic stress disorder (PTSD) assistance, and in some cases family counseling has been made available as the warrior tries to re-assimilate into the community (not enough of the latter, but some well-intentioned efforts). So we see that when we have a system in which the politicians can't blame the war on the troops they sent there, some real positive outcomes can develop. If you think this is exaggerated, go back and review the Sunday talk shows of 1969 through 1975 and count the number of times the host or the guest politician suggests that the troops are responsible for the war. It will amaze you.

The Founding Fathers thought that having an independent and free press was a vital asset to the development of a democratic society. It was as though they had unleashed the dragon when this independent and free press actually got going—one of more than a few surprises they didn't see coming. Once the press was unshackled from the British censor, it became very robust and much more likely to publish what some editors thought rather than just the (alleged) facts of a circumstance or situation. The concept of the investigative free press took a while to evolve. Naturally this produced newspapers with surprising agendas and radical positions. The idea that you could just publish anything you wanted to say with no censor was much abused and often lead to the publication of downright lies. At the time of the Articles of Confederation the esteem of some of the Founders prevented a runaway yellow press, but it developed eventually. By the time of our second president, John Adams, yellow journalism was completely out of control.

This drove Adams to initiate the Alien and Sedition Act. The act was hated by most citizens and was seen as Adams' attempt to reinstitute a censorship and an aristocracy to the original thirteen states, which was probably the main reason he was just a one-term president. But it wasn't entirely wrong-headed; the country was being overrun with special interest agents who had been given money by foreign powers to persuade the population that the foreign policy of the new nation should be aligned with the interests of one or another of the various competing European powers. Does this sound familiar? Adams' real concern was to prevent the country from being misled into a policy that was counter to our real needs. His almost eighteen years of service to his country, in the good times and the bad, had taught him that following the bloodthirsty ways of the new French masters, the Jacobeans, or reattaching the country to the British throne was not in our interest. Although the media had a field day with his laws, he did achieve the removal of these foreign elements from our news media and excluded their influence from our country and restored some sense of civil deliberation to the discussions that were occurring. A much underappreciated effort then and now.

Popular support for a free press was strong as this excerpt from the Philadelphia Freeman's Journal shows:

"As long as the liberty of the press continues inviolate, and the people have the right of expressing and publishing their sentiments upon every public measure, it is next to impossible to enslave a free nation. Men of an aspiring and tyrannical disposition, sensible of this truth, have ever been inimical to the press, and have considered the shackling of it, as the first step towards the accomplishment of their hateful domination, and the entire suppression of all liberty of public discussion, as necessary to its support. For even a standing army, that grand engine of oppression,

if it were as numerous as the abilities of any nation could maintain, would not be equal to the purposes of despotism over an enlightened people. An abolition of that grand palladium of freedom, the liberty of the press, in the proposed plan of government, and the conduct of its authors, and patrons, is a striking exemplification of these observations. The reason assigned for the omission of a bill of rights, securing the liberty of the press, and other invaluable personal rights, is an insult on the understanding of the people."

As mentioned previously there would have been no approval of the Constitution without the Bill of Rights, and there would be no freedom left to us now if our Founders had not included it.

The fact is we still have a decidedly yellow press in this nation, and numerous foreign governments strive to control what we see and hear on our air waves. This is not supposed to be allowed; we have the Federal Communications Commission (FCC) to administer strict laws on media being controlled by foreign interests and by organizations that would seek to control all media in any given region or state. They have, however, completely failed to enforce the law, and the commission chairmen under the Bush administration tried to adjust the commission to allow just a few very powerful and highly moneyed organizations to control all media in all regional and national markets—in effect a national oligarchy for controlled news. He succeeded for the most part; the only reason he didn't completely succeed is that the minority membership on the commission objected because his picks for licensing were entirely Republican and the Democrats on the commission didn't like that. None mentioned the fact that the nation's news would be controlled by just a few individuals who could align it to whatever objective they had. Of course the corporate news never mentioned it either.

This phenomena of federal agencies being taken over by corporations and controlling them has been the death of good public policy and the cause for so many woes among the citizenry that they cannot be enumerated by anyone. The Agriculture Department is completely dominated by the corporate agriculture companies; thus you have them feeding us meats with growth hormones, fattening us up with high fructose corn syrup, a supplement farmers will not even feed to their hogs because it kills them, salt by the ton in everything you buy, and so many chemicals you need a degree in chemistry to even know what they do—and I haven't mentioned fertilizers, pest sprays, and herbicides. All of this from an agency that is supposed to protect our food supply. The same is true in the Education Department, taken over by teachers unions; the Federal Aviation Agency run by the airlines; The Food and Drug Administration, which not only makes sure you pay more for your medications than anyone else in the world, but lets the pharmaceutical companies use you as their guinea pigs for the drugs they sell; the Interior Department, which gave us the Gulf Oil Spill; and the really big one, the Securities and Exchange Commission, which let the Wall Street Bankers run without regulation—the honor system for crooks.

There are unfortunately many, many more federal agencies that have completely gone over to the people they are supposed to regulate, but my point here is this: did you ever get any inkling of their malfeasance before they messed up so badly that it couldn't be kept quiet? So whatever happened to investigative journalism? Could we say that corporate interests might have influenced what you were allowed to know? Do I have to remind you that all of these obvious conflicts of interest are purposely designed to give advantage to the 20 percent over the 80 percent and were put into place by both the Democratic and the Republican parties—a suitable motto of which might be "Citizen be damned; we are going to make some money."

Now we come to the use of politically correct speech by your nightly news anchors. Let's start with a simple one. In 2008, the Russians were said to have invaded a former providence of the old Soviet Union, actually the birthplace of Stalin—Georgia—in the so-called South Ossetia War. Their announced reason was to stop the terrorizing of ethnic Russians in Georgia by the Georgian military. The then president of the United States, George W. Bush, immediately took offense at this and publicly castigated the Russians for this action. In all the media coverage about how there was this very important pipeline that the Russians wanted to control, and how the poor Georgians were being browbeaten by the Russians, and how the brave Georgian leader was defying the Russians, not once in any forum was there a mention of the fact that Georgia started the war, nor just how hypocritical George Bush looked to the rest of the world to be denouncing the Russians while simultaneously conducting two wars of invasion himself. Not once was the word "hypocrite" used on U.S. stations. That is politically correct speech. It is a lie, often of omission, but still a lie. Actually, according to Nicolai N. Petro, professor of politics at the University of Rhode Island, Western media coverage of the war was biased at first but became more balanced in November of 2008 when two OSCE officials, Ryan Grist and Stephen Young, confirmed the Russian version of events—that the Georgian attack was unprovoked and indiscriminate, it was an attempt to "cleanse" the area of Russians. Professor Petro said that initial impressions conveyed by respected news outlets tend to linger on even if the story later changes radically, and "it is therefore not surprising that American pundits and politicians continue to refer to the events of that August as 'Russian aggression,' even though subsequent reporting has debunked this as a myth."

"**I am sure the mass of citizens in these United States mean well, and I firmly believe they will always act well whenever they can obtain a right understanding of matters; but in some parts of the Union, where the sentiments of their delegates and leaders are adverse to the government, and great pains are taken to inculcate a belief that their rights are assailed and their liberties endangered, it is not easy to accomplish this; especially, as is the case invariably, when the inventors and abettors of pernicious measures use infinite more industry in disseminating the poison than the well disposed part of the community to furnish the antidote.**" —President George Washington, letter to John Jay, May 8, 1796

Here's another case of politically correct speech in the media: At the beginning of the political unrest in the Middle East and North Africa, we were told that "investors are nervous and driving up oil prices." As the unrest continued, we were told that "the fear of loss of production from the Libyan oil fields was causing prices to rise." In a little over a month the price of gasoline in this country rose by $0.40 a gallon. What is interesting is the oil production from Libya does not reach our shores. Libya is ranked as seventeenth on the list of world oil producers, below us on the list. Yet every day our gasoline prices were going up. Now I know a thing or two about logistics, and oil tankers just do not move that fast. So if the world price of a barrel of oil was $87/barrel on January 15, 2011, and then was $104/barrel on Feb 1, 2011, the impact of that price rise could not have hit your local pump that fast. You are using gasoline that was actually refined weeks ago. So what is really going on?

As always, the multinational oil companies saw a chance to gouge the American citizen and took it, knowing full well the U.S. government would not act to protect its citizens. But did even one of the national television networks report this truth? I repeat, you are the universal prey; corporations and governments think of you as their own private cash cow.

After the beginning of the first twenty-first-century global depression, the government and the news media magically came up with an unemployment number that was at once ludicrous and insulting. We supposedly had unemployment of a little over 10 percent. Surely everyone in the country knew they were lying through their teeth. Yet the corporate media keeps reporting the government unemployment number like it was truth. So let's take a look at the number as a hypothetical exercise to understand how the government, in this case the US Bureau of Labor Statistics, calculates the unemployment statistics. As an example if 9 million people are out of work and that is 10 percent of the labor force, then we have just 90 million people in the labor force. Right off the bat that seems like a very low number for a country with over 310 million people; and most households have two workers in the family. But the magic starts with a reduction in the population down to 237.8 million based on something called "civilian non-institutional population," which gives us over 72 million people in institutions; I guess. The Bureau of Labor Statistics does not like to define just who the 72 million institutionalized Americans are, but that number would certainly explain why the Medicare population is growing so fast and why the cost of the same is out of control. So now we have 237.8 million Americans in the labor force, but we are informed that 84 million of them are not in the labor force. I think this could be children and elderly, but that is not explained. Of the 84 million, 75 million don't want to work; I suppose we got that information by canvassing them, but canvassing 75 million people is next to impossible, so this is an estimate. That still leaves 9 million who are not in the ranks of the unwilling. Turns out if they didn't look for a job in the past week they are not included in the 9 million. Of course that means they had to actually find a job they were qualified for and apply, so if they couldn't do that they were no longer in the pool; they were no longer in the pool if they got discouraged. But now we have just 153.2 million in the pool and 139.6 million are employed. Again these are the US Bureau of Labor Statistics numbers not mine. That leaves 13.6 million still looking for work, not 9 million. But the Labor Department goes further and tells us that only 6.4 million of those people still want a job. The statistical methods used to come up with this very subjective information is suspect, to say the least, but if you just use common sense and add back in the 9 million listed as not in the labor force who still want a job and the 8 million who are somehow excluded because they are not saying they still want a job (Again it is impossible to canvass 8 million people— the government made this as an estimate.), we don't have 13.67 million unemployed, we have 30.67 million people unemployed. Using the government's base figure, which itself is magically lowered, we would have a rate of 19.93 percent, not 8.9 percent. Remember we haven't even discussed how many are underemployed. If you have had difficulty following this calculation and trying to understand the logic behind it, you have got my point. I apologize for dragging you through this, but sometimes words just don't adequately explain an experience, you have to live it.

So why are corporate media stations reporting on statistics they know are wrong, and why is the government lying? One reason—to keep you emotionally sedated and spending so they can make profits and tax you more without complaint; this is yet another benefit of political correctness.

For many years now we have seen corporations sponsoring cop shows, such as on your corporate media television networks: CBS-Blue Bloods, NBC–Law and Order, FOX-Cops, and ABC-Castle. Indeed, with the exception of ABC, they are almost the only drama programs these networks run. Are you aware that few of them make the Neilson ratings top twenty-five programs? Yet on all of these channels they are practically the only thing to watch between the hours of 7:00 p.m. and 10:00 p.m., prime time, on any given night. I'm sure you see how the crime fighters in all of these programs are saving their communities and keeping us all safe. If your design was to create an acceptance of the idea that we needed to be safe rather than free, what better media than a television blitz of cop shows emphasizing the need for all of us to acquiesce to this police state mentality. I happen to know that jobs other than police work are both dramatic and entertaining, but in prime time America, you will likely not hear of them.

When watching your favorite evening news show, have you ever noticed that all the commercial sponsors are pharmaceutical companies? Do you know they are paying very high rates for those commercials? Are you aware that those kind of commercials are banned in most other first-world countries? Did you ever wonder why?

Psychosomatic medicine is an interdisciplinary medical field studying the relationships of social, psychological, and behavioral factors on bodily processes and well-being in humans and animals. The influence that the mind has over physical processes, including the manifestations of physical disabilities that are based on intellectual infirmities rather than actual injuries or physical limitations is manifested in treatment by the power of suggestion, the use of positive thinking, and concepts like "mind over matter." The academic forebear of the modern field of behavioral medicine, psychosomatic medicine plays a role in psychiatry, psychology, neurology, surgery, allergy, dermatology and psychoneuroimmunology—in short, in any clinical situation where mental processes act as a major factor affecting medical outcomes.

So if you are subjected to a nightly reiteration of pictures showing the bloodstream platelets building up in your blood and demanding that you get a certain medicine or suffer heart attack, how long do you think it will take before your bodily functions start to take this power of suggestion literally and you develop platelets in your blood? Remember it largely subliminal since you would not actually pay a lot of attention to the commercial, but subliminal is all it takes to implant the suggestion, and the rest is history. This is the reason these commercials are band in other countries. But those would be countries that value their citizens more than a buck, that isn't happening here.

Did you ever watch a Sunday morning news program where the host is interviewing a guest on some subject of interest and you keep wondering, "When is he going to ask the question; when is he going to ask the question?" but the question never gets asked? Boy, I sure have. I remember shortly after the Senate passed the prescription drug addition to the Medicare bill in 2007, a principle architect of the bill was interviewed, but no one asked him why the Senate would put in a provision to the bill that stated that the Department of Health and Human Services could not negotiate with the pharmaceutical companies on the price of the drugs being bought through the prescription drug provision. I would certainly have wanted to hear an explanation of that. There are always areas like that in our spotty coverage of the news that just gets left out by the media.

I guess we are supposed to think they forget to ask, but I don't think that is possible; it is endemic in all corporate media broadcasts. Of course, it could be because the pharmaceutical companies sponsor most of our news casts, but I don't want to be a cynic.

Perhaps even worse is when they do ask the question and get a lame answer that leaves you screaming at the interviewers to say something, and they just go on as though they had gotten the answer to their question. Not one of them ever says, "Oh wait a minute, that is the lamest answer I ever heard; are you really going to insult my intelligence and that of my audience with that crap? How about telling us how much so-and-so paid you to vote for that?" That would be real journalism. We just don't get that from corporate news; what we get is politically correct news—there's a big difference.

How do we fix this?

Media freedom verses media responsibility has always been an issue, likely always will be an issue, and isn't going to get fixed by any magic wand, but a few very obvious safeguards would do a lot to improve the situation. One would be some real independence for our media organizations. We created the Federal Communications Commission to ensure that one group, or an oligarchy of groups, could not latch onto the media and control the content. In theory this was an excellent idea, but in practice, as in almost all other federal agencies, it was taken over by the very people it was met to regulate. So now we have television, newspapers, magazines, and radio news sources being controlled by a very few companies or individuals, always elitist aligned, and always bent on making sure you get only the news they want you to know. Ever wonder why ABC, CBS, NBC, and FOX all have their headquarters and their news broadcasts out of New York City just a few blocks from Wall Street? The Elite like to keep close to the vest the vehicles that ensure the continuation of their position as the reigning aristocracy of this nation.

Let's use an analogy. Much like the need for land reform in South America we heard about so frequently during the 1970s and 80s, we must have media ownership reform. If twenty-two families controlled all the land in Peru during the 1960s and 70s and that made everyone else in Peru a serf to those land owners, then it is obvious that we are all serfs to the very few who own all of the news media in this country; we need media ownership reform now. We will only get this reform when the Democrats and Republicans no longer run the government. Voting for them will keep you a serf.

Chapter 4
The Financial Industry: Wall Street vs. Main Street

"Cherish, therefore, the spirit of our people, and keep alive their attention. Do not be too severe upon their errors, but reclaim them by enlightening them. If once they become inattentive to the public affairs, you and I, and Congress, and Assemblies, Judges, and Governors, shall all become wolves." —Thomas Jefferson, letter to Edward Carrington, January 16, 1787

Take a moment and consider the source of the panic bailout of Wall Street in 2008—it came from the Bush administration—from the former CEO of Goldman-Sachs. It is an attempt to roll back the enormous miscalculations of a financial industry that has done nothing but gouge and undermine the American middle class for decades. These are the selfsame people who raise your interest rate on every loan you have the minute you are late on any one of them. They are the ones who bait and switch you into taking a credit card at 3.9 percent interest and then heave that rate up to 36 percent in less than two years, whether you pay on time or not. Then when the payments are so high you can't make them anymore, they sell the right to collect your loan to some criminal who learned his trade working for the Mafia, and he harasses you, hounds you, and threatens you until you are forced to seek the protection of the bankruptcy courts. These are the conmen that sold the American people on adjustable rate mortgages; these are the guys who say that, now that your home is in foreclosure on a 15 percent interest rate, not the 5 percent you started with, they can do nothing to help you. Indeed, they would rather let it foreclose and sit there in ruins than roll back interest rates to help people. This is the gang of criminals who lobbied Congress to change the bankruptcy laws so they could squeeze every last dime out of the people they robbed, deceived, and hoodwinked.

Now even though there is chapter 7 bankruptcy for businesses, it is really only a form of loan consolidation for the serfs. The Republicans, under the Bush administration, even changed the laws to prohibit student loans from coming under the bankruptcy provisions. These are the same people who drove the housing market up to $500,000 homes when people couldn't afford $200,000 homes because they (the financial wizards) lobbied Congress to allow American companies to send our good manufacturing jobs overseas so they could make bigger profits. They said it was globalization, but it was the biggest mass transfer of wealth ever seen. They also got the usury laws dropped in every state with the help of willing, greedy representatives. In short, these are the people who, with Congresses' help, have killed the goose that laid the golden egg and now want that dead goose to bail them out. How can anyone take them seriously?

Now is the time for the American people to stand up to this pack of crooks and finally say *no*. Their panic attempt won't work this time. Remember the Patriot Act and how fear tactics pushed through legislation that gave George

Bush and Dick Chaney more power to run secret prisons, abduct people off the street, and send them to foreign countries to be tortured while their basic rights guaranteed in our Bill of Rights were denied, never mind the fact that this Bush administration was spying on everyone in the country illegally? Don't fall for fear tactics again. The American Middle Class needs to be represented now, not the big corporations, not the special interests, not crooked politicians, but the middle class. We need leaders who will stand up and defend us from these conmen and take action that will make it impossible for them to trample our rights and our economy again.

By now you might have come to the conclusion that I want to bring big business down, that I don't want them around. That would be a mistake. I want American businesses to grow as big as they possibly can; I do want limits on the growth of business enterprise. I'm simply want a level playing field. This is not about American corporations verses foreign corporations, but American companies verses American companies. Every time your congressman gets an earmark put into a bill, he is leveraging one American company over other competing American companies. Is he benefitting his local constituents? Maybe, but more to the point, is he benefitting a company that has made a political contribution to his campaign? I sometimes think that the most politically naive people in all of America are small-business owners, say companies of net worth $10 million or less. Most of these are owned by trade people trying to grab that brass ring. My father was one of them; I have been one of them. I understand when you have an idea, a dream, you focus on that dream and you don't bother yourself with a lot of politics. But sometimes you just have to pull your head out of the sand long enough to be aware of who is with you and who is against you. I see so many of you proudly displaying the chamber of commerce symbol in your businesses and elsewhere, and I wonder if you even have a clue. The chamber of commerce in every city and town in this country only represents the largest corporate entities in the nation. It does not represent small businesses and it never will. The hundreds of paid lobbyists it puts into Washington have no interest in small businesses. Their one objective is to maximize the profits of the largest corporations in the nation. They are not for you, yet you are supporting them. Do I have to tell you that you are not a multinational corporation? Many of you like to think that your coming of age is becoming a Republican, so you loudly espouse the Republican mantra but never seem to stop and think what it means to you and your business. Use your brain. Does cutting all the social benefits of the 80 percent benefit you? Do you gain because they get less? Who are your customers? Consider this:

"Dependence begets subservience and venality, suffocates the germ of virtue, and prepares fit tools for the designs of ambition." —Thomas Jefferson, Notes on the State of Virginia, Query 19, 1787

How is your business ever going to prosper in a nation of surfs? Your big beef with the Democrats is that they like to dump regulations on you like you were a hole and they were a sand truck. You are absolutely right about that, but when did the Republicans ever repeal or even slow down the mountain of bureaucratic paperwork that you get every day? When did they ever give you even one of the benefits they get for their big business clients? When Republicans controlled both houses of Congress and held the presidency in 2007, did your paperwork fiasco even slightly abate? Can you afford to have departments set up in your struggling business just to take care of the paperwork mountain Congress dumps on you? Can you afford to employ the full-time services of accountants, lawyers, secretaries, tax consultants, and financial planners? Your friends in the big corporations can and do. Does that give them an advantage over you? So where is the level playing field?

The engine of the American economy is the enterprise of her citizens, and, in particular, the driving force to create new jobs, expand the economy, and bring innovation to the marketplace comes from small businesses. Yet every administration in the past forty years has focused all its attention on Wall Street and the giant multinational corporations that lobby and buy Congressmen to facilitate their requests for handouts. Now we see the folly of the assumption that "as goes Wall Street, so goes the nation." We went right into the trash barrel. Main Street drives the economy and always has.

If what I say about small business is true, then why would we pursue a policy of rescuing Wall Street in a financial crisis when it is small business that will get us out of our doldrums? I would add that it will not take $700 billion to make this economy turn around, to see real job creation, real innovation in energy and transportation, and a renaissance of American preeminence in scientific and technological advances. What it will take is exactly what no one in the small business community believes will ever come from any Democratic administration. In truth, it has never come from any Republican administration either. It will take relief from government bureaucracies and cheap credit available to the entrepreneur. It will take a focus on Main Street, not Wall Street. This simple truth could drive us to a much quicker and more decisive recovery than any other devise government might employ to stimulate the economy. Yet it will not happen. Your two political parties are incapable of understanding or focusing on this; the moment their Wall Street lobbyist objects, and be sure they will object, such a measure will be killed. Stillborn. That is what this two-party system delivers every time the issue involves Wall Street, yet you keep voting for them. I won't go into the definition of insanity.

The average small business does not succeed (90 percent fail in the first three years) because the average entrepreneurs don't realize when they begin a business that they will spend up to and sometimes exceeding 50 percent of their time working for the bureaucracies that the government(s) has created. Most in Congress do not appreciate this because they have never had to deal with it. Those who have, fled it to get into something else, like politics, where they don't have to deal with it. Yet they are so tied to the party line they can do nothing independently to help entrepreneurs. Worse, it doesn't go away, even when you succeed and remain in business; you still have to work half your waking hours for the government.

Put yourself in these shoes: you're in a small-to average-sized city in the Midwest, it has always been your desire to "make something of yourself," so you started that restaurant you dreamed of, that auto repair shop, that gas station, or that small manufacturing firm. You saved all your life to do this, and you borrowed through every line of credit you could get. You're set to be your own boss; now reality sets in. You hire your first employee. Not less than twenty-six government agencies descend on you. They don't ask you nicely: they demand, they insist, they threaten. You must fill out their paperwork, you must do it in triplicate, and you must send it every week.

Now you have your business. You were right, it was a good idea; customers are coming in the door, and the business is growing. But the larger it grows the more demanding the bureaucracies become, and you hear from more of them. Pretty soon you have hired a lot of help that you did not plan for, nor can you afford, to keep them at bay. That eats into your profits; expensive, accountants, lawyers, and clerks are expensive. Now there is no profit, no hope of expanding the business, no likelihood that you can continue to meet payroll and keep the business going. Your restaurant, your hardware store, your manufacturing plant is just not possible, and you can't compete. The big boys, the Wal-Mart's, the General Motors, the GEs, the Exxon-Mobiles, the ADMs have got armies of clerks, accountants, and lawyers, and they have sent their lobbyist to Washington to join thousands of other lobbyists already there. You can't afford to do that. The government is giving them tax breaks, actually sending them money in some cases: for example, in the aerospace/defense business actually pays for its entire overhead in negotiated rate agreements. You have no chance of getting any of that, so you go out of business.

Now let's say you're part of the rare group of survivors. You are the sole proprietor of your small business; your gift shop is doing well enough to allow you to make a living, but you have to work sixteen hours a day, seven days a week, to keep it going. Instead of going home every night to your family and putting the kids to bed, you are in your small office filling out forms and trying to keep up with the ever-increasing demands of the bureaucracies. You grow old too quickly. You get tired, and you quit the business.

This is the real cost of our system of bureaucratic rule—the stifling of the American free spirit and the limiting of our capacity to express ourselves and create community improvements. This is what has created the urban ghettos we see in our large cities. Those Americans have no resources to win against this mass of government demands. They are beaten before they begin. But the same is true for the small family-owned farm: they are badgered out of business by the very agencies the government says were created to help them. Those agencies now belong—lock, stock, and barrel—to the giant corporate farms who are funded by Wall Street to produce ever more dangerous food supplies with little or no nutrition, covered with insecticides, growth hormones, and preservatives. They have all the loans they need to snap up all the available farmland that is for sale; they get the loans from Wall Street, and the family farmers can't afford to buy the land and expand their production, so they can't win on any bid. They can't market like the corporate farms can either, and they certainly will not get the government largess that Congress appropriates every year for their farmer buddies on Wall Street. You see, the family farmers don't have the team of lawyers it takes to get one of those grants they pass out in the Agriculture Department.

If just one U.S. president did nothing in his or her administration but get control of these bureaucracies that would be a greater accomplishment than what all predecessors combined have done. It is essential to our recovery; these bureaucracies will undermine everything you attempt if we do not flush out the old and install a new team. We cannot allow an entrenched bureaucracy to become our Achilles' heel. Vote every last one of the bums out. No matter how much you like your own senators or congressmen, if they belong to one of our two political parties they are your enemy—they must go.

May I suggest that we issue an executive decree declaring an emergency stop to all bureaucratic demands on any business with less than $10 million dollars in annual revenue? I know that even small business needs regulation, but not stifling regulation that ensures they can't compete and creates an oligarchical rule of the multinational corporations. Give small business a break—a big break—and you will see this economy bloom. I would also suggest that you start a grants program, not a loan program, but a grants program for small businesses engaged in the green revolution. Get them the cash and you will see a much bigger return than you have ever seen from Wall Street or ever will. The fact is that most Wall Street investment firms, like Lehman Bros., have no economic or social function; they are leeches on the backs of every citizen.

Speaking of Wall Street, let's get back to that level playing field. So let's say you are an entrepreneur in a new high-tech venture. You rounded up a considerable amount of startup capital, not from banks, not from the brokerage houses on Wall Street, but from those "angel" investors that hang out in many communities and make their investments the old-fashioned way: they meet with you, they quiz you about your idea, and they take a large share of your company to get you started. That is only fair, and it is the right way to make investments and do business. So now you have a leased space, the equipment you need, and a small amount to pay your employees. But you have staggering odds to overcome to get the right employees; those benefits that the big corporations can offer are nowhere near what you can offer. You have no health insurance, no vision insurance, no dental plan, not life insurance, no disability insurance, no employee savings plan, no IRA. Even if you can buy any of these, you wind up paying three or four times what your established corporate competitor pays. Your chances of getting that highly motivated engineer or technician are just about zero. You can't compete.

You better have all of the technical knowledge you need right inside your own head, or don't even try. But if there were affordable health insurance, vision insurance, dental insurance, and so on that was one price for all, wouldn't that improve your chances? So why do you belong to organizations that lobby to stop that from happening? I know you like a challenge, but this doesn't just place you at a disadvantage: it places the whole country at a disadvantage. That really sharp engineer who took the job with the big corporation will spend his career trying to get his ideas into new products and will have less than a 10 percent chance of that ever happening. Big corporations don't like big ideas; they like very small ideas, the ones that present little or no risk. Big corporations are risk adverse and will always be so. That is why they stagnate and die, or would, if your government didn't bail them out. So that engineer whose idea could change the way we generate energy will never see the idea in action. And that small business that was created to change the way we generate energy will never get the engineer it needs. Know what? The big corporations with their entourage of lobbyist on K Street love it that way.

We think one of the most annoying things is to write your congressmen about some bureaucratic mess, some case of, say, the bureaucrats not crediting your account properly if you have a Sallie Mae loan, or a case of the Social Security administration trying to gouge you for payments they say you owe them when you have just come back from over a year of serving your country in Iraq, and you get a response that, in effect, says, "I can do nothing; it's the federal system and I can't change it." Don't you just want to scream that the Constitution gives them the power of the purse string? Yet these congressmen actually believe that; they really don't know the Constitution, and they are forced into lockstep with their party's rules so thoroughly that they don't know they have the power to stop them cold. That is pathetic.

If one wanted to design a system of economic inequality, the first place to start is to make sure the masses (citizens) are kept in constant fear of losing their livelihood and they are kept completely in the dark about who genuinely has a say in economic decisions. The second step would be to ensure they think they have representatives at the table where the decisions are made without providing actual representation. Next, be sure to bombard citizens with misinformation, half-truths, lies, and subtle forms of acceptance of unequal circumstances. Finally the cornerstone of your inequality system would be to make them believe that some citizens, by virtue of birth, education, or financial situation, are just better able to run things than the rest of the herd. That is how you get and keep a 20–80 skew.

"Democracy will soon degenerate into an anarchy, such an anarchy that every man will do what is right in his own eyes and no man's life or property or reputation or liberty will be secure, and every one of these will soon mould itself into a system of subordination of all the moral virtues and intellectual abilities, all the powers of , beauty, wit and science, to the wanton pleasures, the capricious will, and the execrable cruelty of one or a very few." —John Adams, "An Essay on Man's Lust for Power," August 29, 1763—John Adams

So let's talk a little about our consumer economy. The two political parties want you to understand now that we have gone for globalization as a national goal for both parties, that we are no longer an industrial economy, nor an agrarian economy, nor even a service economy: we are a consumer economy. The parties want you to buy this idea because it will change your expectations about your place in society and your economic outlook. Basically, they do not want you to plan a career in industrial management, agricultural engineering, or even computer services because the grand plan of globalization is that the industrial manufacturing jobs will go to China, the agriculture jobs will be spread out among all the third-world countries, and the service sector jobs will go to India. That leaves you with retail jobs, working for Wal-Mart at minimum wage, with no health insurance, or any other kind of insurance, no pension plan, and no hope of a different future. You can say that is an overstatement all you want, and you can tell me that there is no conspiracy to bring this about, but I really don't have to defend the statement because that is what they are doing in plain sight, right in front to your nose, and so far you haven't really objected; you just keep re-electing them. So what would stop them?

So how do you get to be a member of the American aristocracy? By buying up all the congressmen and senators your pocketbook can afford. Don't worry about bloodlines, just make money anyway you can, and then buy up Congress and have them make laws that give you the advantage in all your business dealings. Not only do you get richer, but you get to buy more congressmen and become even a bigger aristocrat. What a system we have created—does it look like democracy to you!

The Wal-Mart chain followed this simple principle in their business dealings and produced a modern phenomenon—the Wal-Mart economy. Yes, they ran every mom-and-pop store in the country out of business, along with almost all other "big box stores," and completely altered our economy, not to mention our aspirations. You see before there was a Wal-Mart monopoly, there used to be hundreds of thousands of small businesses, maybe even over a million small businesses, that were operated and controlled by individual American entrepreneurs, people who saved their money, got started on a string and a prayer, and made it work. They didn't have any big corporation telling them when to go to work or what they needed to do; they did it themselves. They located their businesses right in your neighborhood, not at the mall, and they sought to make sure they had exactly what you would be shopping for when you came in. You see, they knew you, called you by name, would stop what they were doing to talk to you. They were genuinely interested in you because you were their customer and their livelihood, and they wanted to keep you coming back. I know this concept is amazing to anyone under forty, but that is actually how it worked. Oh yes, and did I mention that they bought products that were American made? How quaint!

Then along comes Sam Walton. He was very ambitious, and he realized that if he could gain an advantage on pricing his goods, he would easily get other business' customers. So that is what he did. At first he just kept expanding his business into ever more markets, and that allowed him to buy in quantity and lower his prices because he had a buying advantage. But then he decided that wasn't enough. You might say he got greedy. He went to the manufacturers and said he wanted to get a special lower price on his purchases than anyone else. He got a lot of them to agree because by now he constituted a large percentage of their business and they couldn't afford to lose him as a customer. By then he had managed to wipe out tens of thousands of those small businesses that didn't have the capital to compete with him. They all got to go to work for someone else and lost their dreams of being independent.

But you know old Sam still had some competitors left and he didn't like that, so he kept squeezing and squeezing his suppliers for lower prices. Finally a lot of them said, "We just can't go any lower; we haven't been able to give our investors a dividend in years, and we can't even give our employees a raise. We have gone as far as we can." As I think you might have guessed, old Sam didn't like that answer, and, true to his character, he cut them off and took his business overseas. He went straight to Taipei, and he got a big boost in his plans because the Taiwanese were willing to work for much lower wages than Americans. So he started buying from them, but even that wasn't good enough—he knew he could do better. So he went straight up to Capitol Hill, purchased dozens of congressmen, and got all the laws changed. He got rid of the import fees; he even got a tax break for corporations relocating to foreign countries, and he moved his corporate profit centers offshore.

This was the last key to making his plan work; he had actually run almost every single mom-and-pop place in the country out of business. All those nice manufacturing jobs that allowed a family to get by with just one wage earner were gone, except maybe in the auto industry because Sam didn't sell autos. This had another benefit for Sam: it created a vast labor pool of marginally employed people who had some managerial expertise and who would work for low wages, very low wages. So Sam hired them to run his stores; he paid them next to nothing, forcing both the mom and the pop to work and leave the kids to wherever they could afford to leave them. A lot of bills for this got picked up by the local communities—both government and private charities. It didn't stop there, though. Sam didn't just pay low wages: he didn't provide any health insurance like the manufacturers he ran out of business, and, of course, he had no retirement plan for his workers either.

Now you may ask why anyone would want to do something like that. You could ask why he was allowed to so completely destroy an economy that was working. The answer is that he and his whole family had become the new American aristocracy. Fully six of the top ten richest people in America were Waltons. Every congressman in America was anxious to get Wal-Mart stores located in their district so they could get their campaign contribution from the Walton's. Sam succeeded beyond his wildest dreams; millions of people who might have enjoyed an independent living worked for a big box store, living from paycheck to paycheck. Manufacturing types were just unemployed; the Chinese and Taiwanese, the people in India and Singapore, the South Koreans and Indonesians had all taken their jobs. Their old hometowns are now called rust buckets, and they get to live on welfare or scrounge for jobs that the millions of illegal aliens are also trying to take. Ah, but not to worry, we have a new word in our vocabulary thanks to old Sam— It's called "globalization," not "sellout." Do you think our Founding Fathers would have liked the Wal-Mart economy we call globalization? Do you think they would have said this is exactly what we thought the benefits of a free society would cause? How about old Adam Smith's book, Wealth of Nations, that so many political aspirants like to quote: do you think that even Smith had this in mind? You know, I doubt it. I read it, and nowhere does it talk about the consumer economy or globalization.

This turn of events arises from the cultural flaw that says one person should be able to do whatever he wants, despite the chaos and catastrophe he causes to everyone else in his community. After all he is an "entrepreneur," and it is his right to destroy whatever it takes to gain his objective, so long as it's hard to define what he's destroying. I think it's time that all of you who are marginally employed, unemployed, or just want to have some independence write a letter to your congressmen and thank them for their support of good old Sam Walton. Why don't you remind your congressmen that we do still have anti-trust and anti-monopoly laws on the books if he would care to enforce them.

I think it is obvious that the globalization plan has a fatal flaw, at least for the United States; the flaw is that on minimum wage with a flat lined wage structure we simply won't have the cash to be consumers. So if the rest of the world is expecting us to buy their manufactured goods, their agriculture produce, and the services they are selling, they are going to be out of luck because in less than one generation we will not be able to buy anything. If in doubt, take another look at the wealth distribution charts in chapter 2 and at the following graph.

Table 6: Disposable Personal Income

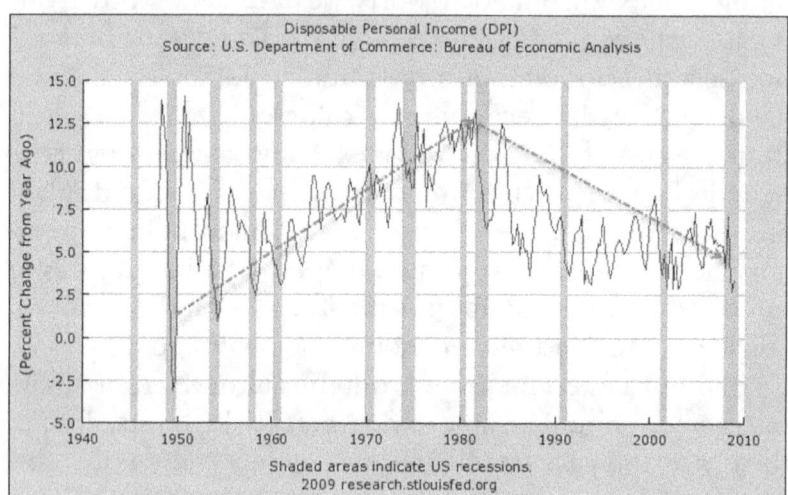

Since the Ronald Regan era of trickle-down economics, the American wage earner has been on a starvation diet. Wages in any terms, be they adjusted for inflation or just compared as though they were in the same period, have absolutely flat-lined. The reason this has happened is that the two parties have conspired with the financial industry to destroy the labor unions. Now I am not a union member and never have been a union member, but even I can see that when a company has 120,000 employees and no union for those employees, the results will be a virtual wage freeze. I know I worked for several of them. The most recent one was an aerospace company that was making record profits due to the fact we are constantly engaged in a war, but used the excuse of the recent depression to say that they were freezing wages for the employees. Now it must be said they didn't make any big public announcements about this; they just did it and took away a holiday, to boot. I guess they figured the employee who doesn't like it can go; the economy is bad and they can pick up another employee easily. So the balance of labor verses management is disrupted. This can happen in any industry. So long as the most important thing on the agenda is how Wall Street will look at your earnings and dividends, then the obvious outcome will be to gouge the employees and pay big dividends. What else would you expect?

Of course the real outcome, if you look past your nose, is that the whole country will experience economic stagnation because that 20 percent does not have the need or the inclination to spend like lower the 80 percent does. Unless you are selling high-end items, your business is going to stand still. Even the aerospace industry could stagnate, but I doubt it; we are too addicted to war to actually pull back from the 157 countries we have a military presence in and to stop spending half of all our GNP on the military and spying on everybody. Remember that the next time a politician tells you that we just have to cut the school budget because they lack the income to provide for it.

I can't really leave this discussion on the balance of labor verses management without mentioning a few salient facts about the American Labor Movement. I think that Americans who work at manual labor jobs owe a great debt of thanks to the American Labor Movement for the fact that they no longer toil in sweatshops, making next to nothing for eighty or even a hundred hours a week; that they actually have rights and some protections is a credit to that movement. I know it is a movement that has experienced a long and steady decline, and it would not be right to just leave it there. My hope is that it is a movement that can be resurrected and brought into the twenty-first century. But there is a lot to overcome in the history of the movement.

Engaging in terror tactics—beating people up, setting up barricades at the workplace, making threats, even killing people or hiring gangsters to enforce your rules, and demanding 100 percent compliance from every worker, and then giving the worker a thug for his union representative will eventually cause some long-term setbacks. What we are seeing with the decline of labor unions is the effective non enforcement of the labor laws on the books, by every American president in the last sixty years, because Wall Street's bought and paid for Congressmen who don't want them enforced, but we are also seeing the inevitable consequences of unrestrained brutality purported by the labor unions on their own members. In short you have a PR problem that is just not going to go away until you stop acting like a bunch of thugs and start focusing on how you can really serve the American Middle Class rather than your own pocketbook. I would suggest you start by looking for real changes to the system that will profoundly even the playing field, and quit thinking like the people who lived 130 years ago. They were only trying to get a chance to survive past the age of forty—we need a different plan now. The new American Middle Class experience will need a strong Labor Movement, but it will not need your archaic thinking.

The management of oligarchical multinational companies is dedicated to the short-term view, and because they have purchased all our legislatures, Congress is also dedicated to the short-term view. Any thought of what may happen if a policy is followed for five or ten years, or what may happen beyond the next election is completely lost on these people. Besides, they will have collected their multi-million-dollar bonuses, and they will have purchased their private island retreats, gained their lifetime benefits, so who cares what happens in ten years? Nevertheless, the advocates of the consumer economy *should* be greatly alarmed by the trends presented in chapter 2; they just can't see it, though, and keep driving us toward that cliff that hangs over the Grand Canyon.

Unless we start looking at a sustainable economy and start changing our nearsightedness for the long view, this economy and this nation will not survive. Smart people everywhere know this. Smart people are not betting on Wall Street to pull us out of anything, and smart people know our government is tied at the umbilical cord to Wall Street so they won't be of any help either. The message here is simple: government created this problem, but they cannot solve it. To do that, we need you.

Now let's talk about antitrust laws. Why would we even have them? Why was Theodore Roosevelt so beloved by his countrymen when he proposed and upheld antitrust laws? Like a lot of reformers, Teddy Roosevelt started small in the totally corrupt political environment of the 1890s in New York State. He managed to get elected because he was one of the elite, an American aristocrat, straight from Wall Street. But he was very much a stealth candidate. Unknown to his fellow Republicans and to the Wall Street crowd, he actually wanted to reform the Tammany Hall politics of New York; he meant what he said in his speeches—he wasn't just lying to get the citizen's vote. This was a great and unpleasant surprise for those who backed him. They solved the problem by sending him to Washington to be undersecretary of the navy, a position which was supposed to bury him. Instead he turned it into a lever bigger than the Washington Monument. Then came the sinking of the USS Maine, and the rest is history. He became our first reformer president since Lincoln, but he wasn't reforming the nation's conscience: he was reforming our financial institutions. He created the antitrust legislation that was the hallmark of the beginning of the twentieth century and the end to the uneven battle between Wall Street and labor unions. Prior to Teddy, whenever and wherever a group of abused and exploited workers got together, they were immediately set upon by the local police forces, arrested, put in jail, and called Communists, and all the political elite, the Political-Financial Complex, made sure the public knew they were trying to tear down American liberty. Exactly how the public bought that is hard to say, but by and large they did.

In Colorado we actually had the National Guard fire cannon on workers engaged in a labor dispute at a coal mine in Trinidad, Colorado. Known as the Ludlow Massacre, this infamous attack wasn't just on striking miners, it was on their wives and children who were living in tents outside the town because the owners of the mine had driven them out of company housing when they went on strike. So we see that state governments are just as culpable in enforcing the two parties, Political-Financial Complex as the national government is. We would see exactly this same atrocity repeated in nearly every state, though probably the worst one would be West Virginia, where at least ten thousand miners and their families were killed by military action in 1907–1908 when they got tired of corrupt politicians and Wall Street Bankers stealing their land with legal tricks to get the coal under it.

Our history since the time of Jackson has been one of incredible abuse of power and destruction of the rights of our citizens to further the aims of Wall Street. The era that followed President Jackson didn't just discriminate against Native American rights to their lands, but against anyone and everyone who didn't belong to the Political-Financial Complex that the two political parties and the elitist faction on Wall Street maintained. They stopped at nothing to keep their advantages over the common citizen, a fact that continues to this day.

"The growing wealth acquired by them [corporations] never fails to be a source of abuses." —President James Madison

An example of the total disregard that the Elitists hold for their fellow Americans and for democracy is the story of how the Federal Reserve System was founded. Because of repeated bank failures throughout the 19th and early 20th century, Americans, especially business owners, were very wary of bankers. Many of the failures were caused by investment abuses or downright embezzlement. Americans were especially fearful of a powerful central bank like those that existed in most European countries. The majority of Americans were immigrants from Europe and had first-hand knowledge of the abuses caused by these banks which included fomenting wars. Thus in 1910 this country still did not have a central bank. However the moguls of Wall Street wanted one. As one of the formulators of the plan stated we now control only the money here in New York but soon we will control all the money in the nation. Thus six men left New York and journeyed to a hunting lodge on Jekyl Island, Georgia. The six men were Senator Nelson Aldritch, head of the National Monetary Commission, Frank Vanderlip, President of the National City Bank of New York, Henry Davison, senior partner of the J.P. Morgan Company, Charles Norton, President of the Morgan owned First National Bank of New York, Benjamin Strong, another Morgan employee, and Paul Warburg, a member of the Warburg and Warburg Bank of Germany and recent partner of Kuhn, Loeb and Company, New York. It was estimated that these men represented 17% of the WORLD's wealth. They are hardly a representative group.

The plan they developed in secret would become our Federal Reserve System when enacted by Congress in 1913. The American people were told that this would end all financial crises. We learned better when something called the Great Depression hit the nation in 1929. Strangely despite repeated economic problems and bank abuses, this system has never been changed nor has any Congress suggested we eliminate it.

HOW DO WE FIX THIS?

In other chapters I have suggested we go to economic boycotts to shut down Wall Street and the Chicago Board of Trade by making them powerless entities, but really we have to make them illegal entities. We need to outlaw lobbying, and we can do this because this is still a democracy; we citizens must make the laws that level the playing field because our current representatives in Congress are certainly not going to do so. We must reinvent our economic system based on a new paradigm. We must stop voting for political parties whose only role in our society is to divide us. Americans are not naturally divided by our outlooks, our race, our religion, our ethnicity, or our economic status; we are divided by those political parties that can only exist if they convince us that we should be separated in this way. These parties are in turn given their mission of maintaining the division among us by the institutions of greed on Wall Street. The parties are not independent and are not bringing together any grassroots movements. They do not attempt to lead us, but rather follow the agenda of others, not galvanizing America's people about a real political or economic cause, but by diverting our attention from the important things that impact us directly with red hearings and deceit. They have absolutely no interest in leading the people or addressing their grievances because that would be an attack on their puppeteers.

First and foremost we fix this by never voting for them again. But we must do more; this elitist mentality has been the tapeworm sapping the energy out of every endeavor this republic has set about for over 120 years. The idea that citizens of a democratic republic would live by exploitation of one group against another is antithetical to the principles set forth in the Declaration of Independence. It destroys community and sets into motion the paranoia that is at the heart of a police state mentality, leaving us with disunity and distrust. Nations do not survive this. Read your history, even if the state doesn't want you to, and see the bleaching bones of hundreds of societies that allowed this to happen and paid the price with extinction.

I know some of you would say that I'm trying to redefine human nature, and I do not disagree with that, but isn't it at long last time we evolved to something better? There is no denying we live on a planet that has, as its main characteristic, a constant preying of one species on the other, but couldn't it be that we are supposed to be the species that finally overcomes the prey instinct and moves to a higher level of existence? The idea is not new. Even if you are not religious, you have to agree that it was expressed very succinctly by St. Paul in his letter to the Romans 8:19: "For all of creation is in anxious longing and eagerly awaits the revelation of the sons of God" and in 8:22: "For we know that the whole creation groans and suffers the pains of childbirth together until now."

We Americans as a people are better than that; we demonstrate it every time we have a natural disaster, every time we hear of an injustice, every time we respond to the need of another. We do not prey on each other, but help each other in the spirit of community and in the spirit of love. I believe this great country of ours was founded to do just that, and it is high time we got on with it.

Chapter 5
Police Power: A Prison Nation

One of the most disturbing developments in our country in the past century has been the rise of a police state. Prior to the 1920s we did not have a national police organization, i.e., the FBI, and prior to World War II we did not have a permanent spy organization like the CIA. Now we have the following:

FEDERAL

DEPARTMENT OF HOMELAND SECURITY (DHS)
United States Coast Guard (USCG)
Coast Guard Police (CGPD)
Coast Guard Investigative Service (CGIS)
United States Customs and Border Protection (CBP)
United States Border Patrol (USBP)
Federal Protective Service (FPS)
United States Immigration and Customs Enforcement (ICE)
United States Secret Service (USSS)
Transportation Security Administration (TSA)
Federal Air Marshal Service (FAMS

DEPARTMENT OF JUSTICE (USDOJ)
Bureau of Alcohol, Tobacco, Firearms, and Explosives (ATF)
Drug Enforcement Administration (since 1973)
Bureau of Narcotics and Dangerous Drugs (1968–73)
Federal Bureau of Narcotics (1930–68)
Bureau of Prohibition (1927–33)
Bureau of Drug Abuse Control (1966–68)
Federal Bureau of Investigation (FBI)
Federal Bureau of Prisons (BOP)
United States Marshals Service (USMS)

DEPARTMENT OF STATE (DOS)
Bureau of Diplomatic Security
Diplomatic Security Service (DSS)
Department of Commerce (DOC)
National Oceanic and Atmospheric Administration Fisheries Office for Law Enforcement

DEPARTMENT OF TREASURY
Internal Revenue Service Criminal Investigations Division (IRS-CID)
Treasury Inspector General for Tax Administration (TIGTA)
United States Mint Police (USMP)
United States Treasury Police (merged into the US Secret Service Uniformed Division in 1986)

DEPARTMENT OF DEFENSE
Defense Criminal Investigative Service (DCIS)
Pentagon Force Protection Agency
Department of the Army
United States Army Criminal Investigation Division (Army CID)
United States Army Military Police Corps

Department of the Air Force

Air Force Office of Special Investigations (Air force OSI)

Air Force Security Forces

Department of the Navy

Naval Criminal Investigative Service (NCIS)

Office of Naval Intelligence Police (ONI Police)

Marine Corps Provost Marshal's Office

Department of Education

Office of the Inspector General (OIG)

DEPARTMENT OF HEALTH AND HUMAN SERVICES

Food and Drug Administration (FDA)

Office of Criminal Investigations

DEPARTMENT OF AGRICULTURE (USDA)

U.S. Forest Service Law Enforcement and Investigations

Office of Inspector General

DEPARTMENT OF THE INTERIOR (USDI)

Bureau of Indian Affairs Police

Bureau of Land Management Office of Law Enforcement & Security

National Park Service

National Park Rangers

United States Park Police

U.S. Fish & Wildlife Service Office of Law Enforcement

Other Major Federal Law Enforcement Agencies

Central Intelligence Agency Security Protective Service (SPS)

Federal Reserve Police

Library of Congress Police

National Security Agency Police (NSA Police)

Smithsonian National Zoological Park Police

United States Capitol Police (USCP)

United States Postal Inspection Service (USPIS)
United States Supreme Court Police
Veterans Affairs Police

I think you would agree that this is quite a proliferation of police agencies. Of course some have very specific focuses and responsibilities that are unique to their particular function, but too many have very broad focus and no limit to their function. One would be the National Security Agency, which spends all day every day violating our Constitution. The government does not have the right to spy on all of its citizens regardless of whether they are under suspicion. The Constitution does not allow for such activity. Let's take a closer look at our Bill of Rights:

We the People of the United States, in Order to form a more perfect Union, establish Justice, insure domestic Tranquility, provide for the common defense, promote the general Welfare, and secure the Blessings of Liberty to ourselves and our Posterity, do ordain and establish this Constitution for the United States of America.

ARTICLES in addition to, and Amendment of the Constitution of the United States of America, proposed by Congress, and ratified by the Legislatures of the several States, pursuant to the fifth Article of the original Constitution.

Note: The following text is a transcription of the first ten amendments to the Constitution in their original form. These amendments were ratified December 15, 1791, and form what is known as the "Bill of Rights."

Amendment I
Congress shall make no law respecting an establishment of religion, or prohibiting the free exercise thereof; or abridging the freedom of speech, or of the press; or the right of the people peaceably to assemble, and to petition the Government for a redress of grievances.

Amendment II

A well regulated Militia, being necessary to the security of a free State, the right of the people to keep and bear Arms, shall not be infringed.

Amendment III

No Soldier shall, in time of peace be quartered in any house, without the consent of the Owner, nor in time of war, but in a manner to be prescribed by law.

Amendment IV

The right of the people to be secure in their persons, houses, papers, and effects, against unreasonable searches and seizures, shall not be violated, and no Warrants shall issue, but upon probable cause, supported by Oath or affirmation, and particularly describing the place to be searched, and the persons or things to be seized.

Amendment V

No person shall be held to answer for a capital, or otherwise infamous crime, unless on a presentment or indictment of a Grand Jury, except in cases arising in the land or naval forces, or in the Militia, when in actual service in time of War or public danger; nor shall any person be subject for the same offence to be twice put in jeopardy of life or limb; nor shall be compelled in any criminal case to be a witness against himself, nor be deprived of life, liberty, or property, without due process of law; nor shall private property be taken for public use, without just compensation.

Amendment VI

In all criminal prosecutions, the accused shall enjoy the right to a speedy and public trial, by an impartial jury of the State and district wherein the crime shall have been committed, which district shall have been previously ascertained by law, and to be informed of the nature and cause of the accusation; to be confronted with the witnesses against him; to have compulsory process for obtaining witnesses in his favor, and to have the Assistance of Counsel for his defense.

Amendment VII

In Suits at common law, where the value in controversy shall exceed twenty dollars, the right of trial by jury shall be preserved, and no fact tried by a jury, shall be otherwise re-examined in any Court of the United States, than according to the rules of the common law.

Amendment VIII

Excessive bail shall not be required, nor excessive fines imposed, nor cruel and unusual punishments inflicted.

Amendment IX

The enumeration in the Constitution, of certain rights, shall not be construed to deny or disparage others retained by the people.

Amendment X

The powers not delegated to the United States by the Constitution, nor prohibited by it to the States, are reserved to the States respectively, or to the people.

Now read the Fourth Amendment. Ask yourself how it is legal for the NSA to listen in on every conversation being conducted in private on our phone lines? How is it legal for TSA to sexually attack you at airports? What are they thinking? As legal officers don't you know what sexual assault is? If you don't let me give it to you right out of the law: Sexual assault refers to an assault of a sexual nature on another person. It can include a wide range of unwanted sexual contact such as rape, forced vaginal, anal or oral penetration, forced sexual intercourse, <u>inappropriate touching</u>, forced kissing<u>, child molestation</u> ,exhibitionism, voyeurism, obscene phone calls, torture of a victim in a sexual manner etc. <u>The actor causes submission of the victim by means that is reasonably calculated to cause submission against the victim's will. Definitions of offences are primarily governed by state criminal laws, which vary by state. It is generally a felony</u>. This asinine idea of sexually assaulting airline passengers is an idiot's idea. There is a word in the English language that is identified with this nonsense, it is "reactionary". The word reactionary is defined as: "marked by, or favoring reaction, especially in politics, a reactionary person". A completely unbalanced person from Africa goes to Yemen and is persuaded to put a suicide bomb in his underpants and fly to the United States to blow up his airplane on approach to the airport. From that we get 300 million people being molested every time they get on an airplane. If that isn't reactionary I don't know how else it could be defined. It goes without saying that we don't want reactionary people running our nation. How can they go along with this? What does this say to our children? What are we teaching them about who they are? If I did what your Secretary of Homeland Security is having the TSA do, I would immediately be arrested. Let's see, does that make me a fourth-class or a fifth-class citizen? When is the government going to stop treating us like serfs? Janet Napolitano and her henchmen in the TSA need to be immediately fired for even suggesting this nonsense, let alone doing it. Actually, they should be arrested.

Any Constitutional lawyer must know that these body searches violate the Fourth Amendment. They must know this is absurd in any state that believes in liberty. I'm sorry, Mr. President, but we did not found this nation on the idea that we were going to be secure: we founded it on the idea we were going to be free. This nonsense violates every principle that the foundations of this country are built on. You are telling us it's alright for your Brown Shirts to do whatever they want to do to us, but we had better not do the same. What hypocrisy. The Fourth Amendment to the US Constitution states, "The right of the people to be secure in their persons, houses, papers, and effects, against unreasonable searches and seizures, shall not be violated, and no Warrants shall issue, but upon probable cause, supported by Oath or affirmation, and particularly describing the place to be searched, and the persons or things to be seized."

This amendment requires a warrant for arrests and to searches of persons, homes, and other private places. It thereby places a neutral magistrate between the police and citizens.

The Fourth Amendment to the US Constitution provides protection against unreasonable searches and seizures. The amendment specifically requires search and arrest warrants be judicially sanctioned and supported by probable cause. Searches and arrests must be limited in scope according to specific information supplied to the issuing court. That information is usually provided by a law enforcement officer who has sworn by it.

The Supreme Court has also ruled that certain searches and seizures violated the Fourth Amendment even when a warrant was properly granted. The Fourth Amendment specifies that, to be considered reasonable, all search and arrest warrants must be legally sanctioned. The Fourth Amendment only applies to governmental agencies. It does not guarantee a right to be free from unreasonable searches and seizures conducted by private citizens or organizations. Though, the Bill of Rights originally only restricted the power of the federal government, in *Mapp v. Ohio[iv]*, the Supreme Court ruled that the Fourth Amendment is applicable to state governments by way of the Due Process Clause of the Fourteenth Amendment.

The reasonableness requirement of the Fourth Amendment applies not only to a search in combination with a seizure, but also to a search without a seizure, as well as to a seizure without a search. As a general rule, the government may not detain an individual even momentarily without reasonable suspicion. There are however a few exceptions to the rule of reasonableness. In cases when the need of the society is great and to effectively meet the needs of the society, if a minimal intrusion on people's privacy is required; such intrusions can be made. In Michigan v. Sitz[v], the Supreme Court allowed sobriety checkpoints and in United States v. Martinez-Fuerte[vi]; the Supreme Court allowed immigration checkpoints.

The security crowd of paranoid control freaks was running the Bush administration and using 9/11 as an excuse to dump the Bill of Rights, and I'm sure you know that we would not even have had a Constitution, or a nation for that matter, without the Bill of Rights. The very last thing I thought a president who was a Constitutional scholar would do, would be to allow this kind of idiocy to prevail. Do those progressive-revisionists in the Democrat Party think this is good policy? Do they really think it is best to create a police state to defeat terrorism? Surely they know they are letting terrorists win. The only thing they have to sell is fear and Barack Obama and George Bush caved right into them.

Ben Franklin said it best: **"Any society that would give up a little liberty to gain a little security will deserve neither and lose both."**

"The problem in defense is how far you can go without destroying from within what you are trying to defend from without." —President Dwight Eisenhower. The problem here is that both Bush and Obama are listening to legal "experts" like Mr. John Yoo, who were taught in their college classrooms that the Constitution is irrelevant. And they spend all day every day making it irrelevant by ignoring it, though they really don't have to worry about that because we now have a Supreme Court that is made up of justices who are 100 percent Ivy League graduates, taught the exact same thing in their college classrooms.

Regarding the decrease in liberties, perhaps you are thinking we are in a War on Terrorism and have to do everything in our power to win. If we were talking about the Nazi war machine of the 1940s, I would completely agree with you, but I still would not let Franklin D. Roosevelt get away with interning American citizens without cause or charges. We are not facing the Nazi war machine; we are facing a bunch of criminals, funded by our good friends the Saudis, to terrorize us. Their saying they are doing it for their religion does not change a thing. To paraphrase Mark Twain, you could float all the navies of world on the blood spilt in the name of religion. To immediately suspend the Bill of Rights in the American Constitution for the sake of a pack of depraved Muslim dropouts is a travesty. Your Congress gave you, the American citizen, a vote of no confidence, and it gave that to our police as well. If you believe they did it to stop the terrorists, you need to work on your inductive reasoning skills.

As we move toward the cherished globalization goals of our two political parties, they know it will be necessary to remove any Constitutional guarantees from all citizens except themselves. They always exempt themselves. At some point you have to recognize that these constant wars are no accident, and our election as the global policemen is not a choice the American citizen is going to be allowed to refute. Our political parties are in this for the power, money, and glory, and the citizen be damned. And damned we are; we are the serfs in the Elite's new global order.

I know some of you think this is an exaggeration; our political parties would not sell out to a "new global order." If you think this you simply have not attended a class at Harvard or Yale were it is taught openly, you have not been listening to what every president we have had since John F. Kennedy had to say; you are in denial because you want to believe in the promise of our Constitution, not in what our current political systems are demonstrating. This is systemic, and it goes directly against what all of us were taught our country stood for. Here are just a few of the embarrassing situations we have seen come to light on the international stage that show our government is operating in a way to utterly refute any talk of, **"We hold these truths…"**.

"The means of defense against foreign danger historically have become instruments of tyranny at home." — James Madison

In the most comprehensive investigation to date of health professionals' involvement in the CIA's enhanced interrogation program (EIP), Physicians for Human Rights has uncovered evidence that indicates the Bush administration conducted illegal and unethical human experimentation and research on detainees in CIA custody. The apparent experimentation and research appear to have been performed to provide legal cover for torture, as well as to help justify and shape future procedures and policies governing the use of the "enhanced" interrogation techniques. The PHR report, "Experiments in Torture: Human Subject Research and Evidence of Experimentation in the 'Enhanced' Interrogation Program," is the first to provide evidence that CIA medical personnel engaged in the crime of illegal experimentation after 9/11, in addition to the previously disclosed crime of torture.

This evidence indicating research and experimentation on detainees opens the door to potential additional legal liability for the CIA and Bush-era officials. There is no publicly available evidence that the Department of Justice's Office of Legal Counsel determined that the alleged experimentation and research performed on detainees was lawful, as it did with the "enhanced" techniques themselves. "The CIA appears to have broken all accepted legal and ethical standards put in place since the Second World War to protect prisoners from being the subjects of experimentation"' said Frank Donaghue, PHR's CEO **"Not only are these alleged acts gross violations of human rights law, they are a grave affront to America's core values."**

Physicians for Human Rights demands that President Obama direct the Attorney General to investigate these allegations and, if necessary, prosecute those responsible. Additionally, Congress must immediately amend the War Crimes Act (WCA) to remove changes made to the WCA in 2006 by the Bush administration that allow a more permissive definition of the crime of illegal experimentation on detainees in U.S. custody. The more lenient 2006 language of the WCA was made retroactive to all acts committed by U.S. personnel since 1997.

"In their attempt to justify the war crime of torture, the CIA appears to have committed another alleged war crime—illegal experimentation on prisoners," director of PHR' "Justice Department lawyers appear to never have assessed the lawfulness of the alleged research on detainees in CIA custody, despite how essential it appears to have been to their legal cover for torture."

PHR's report, "Experiments in Torture," is relevant to current national security interrogations, as well as Bush-era detainee treatment policies. As recently as February, 2010, President Obama's then director of national intelligence, Admiral Dennis Blair, disclosed that the United States had established an elite interrogation unit that will conduct "scientific research" to improve the questioning of suspected terrorists. Admiral Blair declined to provide important details about this effort.

"If health professionals participated in unethical human subject research and experimentation, they should be held to account," stated Scott A. Allen, MD, a medical advisor to Physicians for Human Rights and lead medical author of the report. "Any health professional who violates their ethical codes by employing their professional expertise to calibrate and study the infliction of harm disgraces the health profession and makes a mockery of the practice of medicine."

Several prominent individuals and organizations in addition to PHR will file a complaint this week with the U.S. Department of Health and Human Services' Office for Human Research Protections (OHRP) and call for an OHRP investigation of the CIA's Office of Medical Services.

The PHR report indicates that there is evidence that health professionals engaged in research on detainees that violates the Geneva Conventions, The Common Rule, the Nuremberg Code and other international and domestic prohibitions against illegal human subject research and experimentation. Declassified government documents indicate that:

Research and medical experimentation on detainees was used to measure the effects of large-volume waterboarding and adjust the procedure according to the results. After medical monitoring and advice, the CIA experimentally added saline, in an attempt to prevent putting detainees in a coma or killing them through over-ingestion of large amounts of plain water. The report observes: "'Waterboarding 2.0' was the product of the CIA's developing and field-testing an intentionally harmful practice, using systematic medical monitoring and the application of subsequent generalizable knowledge."

Health professionals monitored sleep deprivation on more than a dozen detainees in 48-, 96-, and 180-hour increments. This research was apparently used to monitor and assess the effects of varying levels of sleep deprivation to support legal definitions of torture and to plan future sleep-deprivation techniques.

Health professionals appear to have analyzed data, based on their observations of twenty-five detainees who were subjected to individual and combined applications of enhanced interrogation techniques, to determine whether one type of application over another would increase the subject's "susceptibility to severe pain." The alleged research appears to have been undertaken only to assess the legality of the enhanced interrogation tactics and to guide future application of the techniques.

"Experiments in Torture: Human Subject Research and Experimentation in the 'Enhanced' Interrogation Program" is the most in-depth expert review to date of the legal and medical ethics issues concerning health professionals' involvement in researching, designing, and supervising the CIA's program. The report is the result of six months of investigation and the review of thousands of pages of government documents. It has been peer-reviewed by outside experts in the medical, biomedical, and research ethics fields, legal experts, health professionals, and experts in the treatment of torture survivors.

"Only a virtuous people are capable of freedom. As nations become corrupt and vicious, they have more need

of masters." —Benjamin Franklin, letter to the Abbes Chalut and Arnaud, April 17, 1787

The memos provide a detailed glimpse into the thinking of President Bush's Justice Department legal advisors at a time of national emergency. They embraced the view that the president, acting alone, had the authority to override the other branches of government on a broad range of issues. The Justice Department's Office of Legal Counsel, in a memo written six weeks after the Sept. 11, 2001, terrorist attacks, would have allowed U.S. troops to search houses and seize suspected terrorists without a court-approved warrant. The Pentagon never used that power, although it considered it, according to a former Bush administration lawyer.

In the immediate aftermath of the attacks, Justice Department lawyers also said the military's need to go after terrorists in the United States could override constitutional protections guaranteeing the right to free speech. By then, the memos show, the Bush administration was already discussing ways to wiretap U.S. conversations without warrants and to take other steps without the traditional oversight of Congress and the courts.

"The practice of arbitrary imprisonments have been, in all ages, the favorite and most formidable instruments of tyranny." —Alexander Hamilton, Federalist #84

Another memo said the president could unilaterally abrogate treaties with other nations. The memos also showed that five days before Bush left office, the Justice Department issued a secret but remarkable retraction of some of these same sweeping definitions of presidential authority.

In a January 15 "memorandum for the files," Principal Deputy Assistant Attorney General Steven G. Bradbury said many of the Office of Legal Counsel opinions issued between 2001 and 2003 no longer reflected the views of the Justice Department and "should not be treated as authoritative for any purpose." The Justice Department had secretly withdrawn some of its more controversial legal memos years earlier, Bradbury added, "and on several occasions we have already acknowledged the doubtful nature of these propositions."

The memos released more recently still go well beyond what was known about the Bush administration's assertion of presidential power.

Who would have guessed that an attack on the United States would have led to the suspension of our rights as a free people? Or that it would lead to conspiracy, perjury, murder, and theft? These things do not happen haphazardly, nor do they happen in a vacuum. They result from attitudes and beliefs that are left unchecked by better, nobler impulses. They result from a sense of entitlement and egocentrism. Thus, a crime of rage is often an outcome of habitual thought patterns and selfish behaviors run amok. On one level, this story is about the tendency of powerful people to take what they want whenever and however they want it. On another level is about that 20 percent and their determination to have the promises of the American Revolution for themselves alone.

"In these sentiments, Sir, I agree to this Constitution, with all its faults,—if they are such; because I think a general Government necessary for us, and there is no form of government but what may be a blessing to the people, if well administered; and I believe, farther, that this is likely to be well administered for a course of years, and can only end in despotism, as other forms have done before it, when the people shall become so corrupted as to need despotic government, being incapable of any other." —Benjamin

Franklin, speech to the Constitutional Convention, June 28, 1787

Suggestibility can have grave consequences, especially in the setting of the police interrogation room. Forensic psychologists became interested in the power of suggestion in the 1970s, following a series of high-profile cases in which the police where accused of unfairly extracting confessions from suspects. Individuals were convicted on evidence from confessions that were elicited by dubious means and spent years in jail before their convictions were overturned on appeal. At the root of these appeals was the state of mind in which the confessions were made. The subjects were told time and again that they had committed these crimes, and eventually a few of them started to wonder if it really might be true. On some occasions, suspects were allegedly also deprived of sleep, light, and food and were beaten. Had the suspects been so susceptible that they just parroted what the police wanted to hear? In certain cases, this appeared to be true. The suspects later reported that they were no longer sure exactly what they had done or where they had been at the time that the crime was committed.

Police interrogators know how to exploit the situation. Barrie Irving of the UK Police Foundation noted, **"The principal psychological factor contributing to a successful interrogation is privacy, being alone with the person under interrogation."** (A successful interrogation in this context is one that ends with a confession.) Under such conditions some suspects become more suggestible, even though they know that eventually they may be convicted of a crime.

You may think this interrogation policy refers to extracting information from prisoners in our "War on Terror," but it actually describes the general practice of every community police force in the nation. Without any constitutional authority to do so, the Police Protective Association and the commanders and trainers of our police forces have declared themselves above the law. They lie to, deceive, and isolate any person they deem to be a suspect in their investigations; they detain them with lies, denying them access to a lawyer. They get warrants from the courts without a shred of evidence. They spit on the Constitution and try to undermine it at every step. What is more, they are getting away with it because the district attorneys and the courts just give them a wink and a pat on the back. They have placed themselves above the citizens of this country, relegating the 80 percent to 2nd-class citizens, and they know it. If the police shoot someone in their custody, even a handcuffed individual, they are exonerated by the courts. The citizens think this is justified because the police have such difficult jobs. They are willing to give a "not guilty" verdict on anything they do, somehow never seeing that they could be next. They buy the idea of "super citizen" to the detriment of the rest of the community and to the detriment of their freedom, of their children's freedom, and their grandchildren's freedom, then walk away feeling satisfied in this destruction of our delicate system of checks and balances. They actually believe it will never happen to them. That is just sad because the two political parties are not the only ones dismantling the Constitution. As for difficult jobs, is running into a burning building, facing an army of overwhelming force while you defend a village, standing on the deck of a fishing boat in the Bering Straits, or going down in a coal mine in West Virginia when the owner has ignored all the safety inspectors' recommendations any less difficult? I don't see juries giving these people any breaks.

As for the courts themselves, how many people are sitting in jail cells in this country who are innocent? Why does it take so long to get a new trial when you have evidence of innocence? Our courts, particularly the state supreme courts, have established rules of procedure that only build on the injustice of the system, unless, of course, you belong to the 20 percent: then things are expedited. It is the courts that accentuate the class divisions of this supposedly classless society. That any innocent person is sitting behind bars is abhorrent, but that he sits there while people know he is likely innocent is treason. Courts who ignore sloppy work by police labs notorious for finding the evidence the DA wants, courts that allow "expert witnesses" who have been proven wrong on most occasions, courts who invest in prisons and then make sure they are full, all of these abuses have turned up in recent years, yet there are no prosecutions. We are left with "super citizens," immune from the law and from the application of justice.

"At the establishment of our constitutions, the judiciary bodies were supposed to be the most helpless and harmless members of the government. Experience, however, soon showed in what way they were to become the most dangerous; that the insufficiency of the means provided for their removal gave them a freehold and irresponsibility in office; that their decisions, seeming to concern individual suitors only, pass silent and unheeded by the public at large; that these decisions, nevertheless, become law by precedent, sapping, by little and little, the foundations of the constitution, and working its change by construction, before any one has perceived that that invisible and helpless worm has been busily employed in consuming its substance. In truth, man is not made to be trusted for life, if secured against all liability to account." —Thomas Jefferson, letter to Monsieur A. Coray, Oct 31, 1823

We are overdue for corrections to our police force, legal system, and courts, yet these corrections do not happen because the two-party system is not invested in justice but in keeping the status quo. So long as the two parties run our local, state, and national governments, justice will not be found.

But there are two sides of justice and we have failure on the other side as well. Precisely because of the failure of our police forces, I do not ordinarily favor the death penalty, but now we have, sitting in our prisons, individuals who can never make any contribution to this society or to any community. Quite the opposite, they can only hurt and destroy. Yet we taxpayers are paying our hard-earned dollars to keep them alive, to keep their defense attorneys in expensive suits, and to invest in building more prisons. The first and the most significant class of these persons are those prey on children. We have the perfect biblical imperative in Mathew 18:6: "But whoever causes one of these little ones, who believe in me to stumble, it is better for him that a heavy millstone be hung around his neck , and that he be drowned in the depths of the sea." Unfortunately, the pedophiles in this country have no reason to fear drowning, but they should. Given the propensity of our police to seek a conviction over the truth, I would not suggest we throw them into the sea on the first offense, or even the second, but by the third time, it is finished, and we need to remove them from the planet and stop having the taxpayers foot the bill to keep them alive. The same is true of serial killers, serial rapists, killers for hire, killers of family members, and all people who refuse to stop causing serious harm to others. Our children first and foremost must be protected, and we the taxpayers should not be forced to house these predators while they plot their next atrocity; they need the death penalty and justice must be swift. There is a person on death row in California, for example, who killed two coworkers, his wife, his mother-in-law, his wife's two sisters, and two of his own three children. He admitted his guilt and left no doubt as to who did it in his trail of crime, yet has no remorse. The state of California has held him in prison for over twenty years, charging the taxpayers for his keep and never carrying out his sentence. That is malfeasance of office and is a crime against the citizens of that state.

In 2007 there was an incident at Duke University of a Lacrosse team having a party to celebrate their season. Prostitutes either were invited to perform a strip tease act or showed up to get free beer and some clients. (Exactly why was never made clear.) One of the prostitutes, who had some serious mental instability issues, was insulted by the drunken crowd of rowdy college boys while she was performing a strip tease and went to the police stating she was gang raped to get revenge. The prosecutor investigated the charges and decide to arrest the young men and charge them, even though he knew the prostitute was mentally unstable and there were no other witnesses to the alleged gang rape despite the room being full of Lacrosse players and their guests. He later found out he had no DNA evidence either; in fact he had DNA evidence that would exonerate the college boys. His motive to prosecute them was that he was up for reelection and wanted to make a strong statement to the community that he was acting to combat the rowdy student population in the town. The accusation and subsequent suspension from school of the five suspects completely destroyed their reputations and their hoped-for careers. This story would have ended there, and these defendants would have spent the next ten to twenty years of their lives in jail and would have been branded as sex offenders for the rest of their lives, but their parents belonged to the 20 percent. That meant they could afford to hire good legal representation, get independent investigators to look at the evidence, and pull strings to get the state's attorney general to look into it. Eventually the false accusations and the malicious prosecution of the case was overturned. The DA was censured by the North Carolina Bar association and deprived of his license to practice law in that state. Does anyone doubt what would have happened to the accused if they had been part of the 80 percent? Still think we have secured justice for all?

From this corrupt legal system and from the corrupt political system have flowed all the laws that now oppress and undermine the middle class of America. The concept from the beginning was to create a body of social law that was geared to what can only be called the lowest common denominator (LCD). LCD social law placed everyone in the same bracket, and the media pounced on it as an easy way to expound public policy. So if two unstable people have a child, for example, and they subsequently abuse that child with sadistic torture and sexual abuse, then we have to have a law to stop this. No doubt this is true. The media promotes how terrible this abuse has been and how awful and depraved these two individuals are, and then we have Congress acting heroically to stop this abuse. They make a nationwide law concerning child abuse that covers everything from spanking to telling your teenager no they can't go to that rave party, and parents are tied up in knots on how to correct and raise their child. The government creates yet another taxpayer funded agency to come and investigate you if anyone, including your children, say you are not a good parent. Many of the states now have laws that allow children to sue parents, and the media loves to jump on accusations and broadcast them throughout the state and the country. However, if you are found innocent, they will never publish that.

The problem with this kind of lawmaking is (1) It does not stop abuse of children in the least—the abusive parent will still abuse. (2) It stops good parents from acting on their knowledge and instincts to correct and guide their wayward child. (3) It creates an atmosphere of despair in the parent and the child. You can't take the slightest risk of losing your child to a pack of do-not-care bureaucrats who will place the child in a foster home and drug them up until they don't know their own name. Then they forget about him/her. Social engineering promoted by the progressive revisionists has wreaked havoc on our families and our society; it is the bane of any attempt to restore a social order that is civil and responsive. The very politicians who promote these laws are the abject example of what results from this meddling in the family structure. They simply find it impossible to be civil or responsive to anything that doesn't agree with them—a skill in manners and thought they should have developed in childhood.

My point here is not that we should let people get away with child abuse; that would be a moral abdication that is completely unacceptable. Our children are the future and we must do everything we can to protect them. The truth is we do far too little. The point here is that the social engineering of the LCD laws has dire and continuing consequences for everyone and must be stopped. These laws must be repealed.

This discussion of these LCD laws is one that we did not want to take up; as in any situation involving humans you cannot know the innocents or guilt of any person caught up in hurting children. But we decided to talk about it because all too often we see an attitude in the community that assumes the guilt as soon as the media report it. Worse we see the real indifference to what happens to the child almost as though they were guilty too. All I can say is wait until it's your child, your family, and your reputation, and then see if the assumption of guilt is a fair supposition.

Ask any police officer, in any community, and he or she will tell you that you cannot stop a homicide; you do not know who is in danger or when and where the perpetrator may act. So any expectation that our police force will succeed in stopping homicides in our communities is completely misplaced. Perhaps if there is a stalker situation in which the victim knows he or she is in danger, effective police action can prevent a homicide, but all too often it doesn't. We'll examine the reason for that later in this book. So LCD laws accomplish nothing to establish and maintain the safety of children or any other group in the nation, but they do undermine and subvert the family unit that is the bedrock of our country.

How do we handle those who are abusive? We have laws against torture, abuse, and sadism. We enforce these laws at the local level, not the national level, and we equip our police officers with the training and the understanding of what to look for. These criminals have no right to cause our nation to create laws that undermine the family and put an army of bureaucrats on the tail of every citizen with a family so we can say we are dealing with a social problem. Again we see the Nazi attitude of letting the government run the family and telling it how to handle every domestic problem because government agents are better than average people. They have law degrees to prove it. Amazingly the child abuse problem was not so prevalent before we had social engineering LCD laws to prevent it. Of course the media will say that it was underreported, but I grew up in a small town that did not record its first rape in the history of the town until the middle 1960s. It was, of course, the talk of the town and thought to be a most horrible thing. Unfortunately, today it does not even make the news. Child abuse is only one example of the impact of progressive revisionist social engineering LCD laws; I could fill volumes with examples of how this belief system is destroying our society.

My point here is not to try and write the body of law we need to operate a sane society with values and common sense; my point is that operating a society with a two-party system that is compromised by ideologues who have no common sense is insane.

HOW DO WE FIX THIS?

We have to take away the cloak of invincibility from our police, prosecutors, and judges. We have to sue them, prosecute them, and dismiss them for malfeasance. We have to limit their terms of office in every place and level, including the Supreme Court. Failure to do this will only leave us with what we have—a completely corrupt system without any responsibility to the community. That we as citizens have allowed this to go on for so long only speaks to how easily we are divided and how much we need to be united. We are not a third-world country; we should not have corruption ruling us and judging us. But nothing is ever going to change this picture so long as we have the Democratic and Republican parties running the show.

"America will never be destroyed from the outside. If we falter and lose our freedoms, it will be because we destroyed ourselves." —Abraham Lincoln

Chapter 6
Foreign Policy

When you think of America, there are certain attributes that should always come to the fore, attributes like free, just, equal, brave, peaceful, generous, and honest. Americans who have not identified with a particular political party really want these attributes to define America; however, the rest of the world seems to hold that we are not living up to our pretentious claims. Attributes like greedy, overbearing, ruthless, oppressive, self-serving, cowardly, unfair, arrogant, and hypocritical are the ones we have acquired over the years, especially since the Vietnam War. It can be a great blessing to see ourselves as others see us. Clearly there is a large gap between what we want to believe about ourselves and what others believe about us. The reason for this discrepancy lies in our foreign policy.

It isn't new, but the recent overthrow of the dictators in the Middle East and North Africa is again a cause for us to reflect on how very different our values are from our foreign policy. It might also be a time for us to realize how much we have departed from our values at home, not just in the rest of the world. America was once thought to be that shining beacon on the hilltop that lighted the way for the rest of world. When did we extinguish that light? Why have we so often found common cause with the ruthless dictators of the world and not with the suffering humanity that they so heinously control? Remember this poem by Emma Lazarus:

The New Colossus

Not like the brazen giant of Greek fame,
With conquering limbs astride from land to land;
Here at our sea-washed, sunset gates shall stand
A mighty woman with a torch, whose flame
Is the imprisoned lightning, and her name
Mother of Exiles. From her beacon-hand
Glows world-wide welcome; her mild eyes command
The air-bridged harbor that twin cities frame.
"Keep ancient lands, your storied pomp!" cries she
With silent lips. "Give me your tired, your poor,
Your huddled masses yearning to breathe free,
The wretched refuse of your teeming shore.
Send these, the homeless, tempest-tost to me,
I lift my lamp beside the golden door!"

Amazing how much can be said about a place or its people in such a short poem; it's sad that the place and the people have lost so much in the past fifty years. As I'm sure you know, these words are on the pedestal of the Statue of Liberty in New York's harbor. They do give one pause; I just wish the reflection they inspire wasn't so disgraceful.

Billions of taxpayer dollars going to overtly dictatorial governments propped up by our shameless support—is this what we as Americans want to say to the rest of the world? Is this what we are? Did you, like me, buy it when your government told you we had to do that so they wouldn't fall into Communists' hands during the Cold War? The Cold War ended and now the government says we have to do this to keep world peace and world order. Do you see any peace in the world, and exactly who's order are we keeping? Certainly not the suffering humanity we claim to love. Does this duplicity ever end? Even if you are taught all your life that the new world order our politicians are building for humanity is the right thing, can't you even foster an original thought about what the cost of this is, and how do we justify that? Have you rationalized so much that you can't find truth? If so, at least you aren't the first to do it; the whole nation of Germany was doing it from 1935 until 1945, when they couldn't do it anymore. Truth will out.

After the Second World War the U.S. government found itself in a very powerful position. Effort was made then to use this position to leverage a more peaceful world. The United Nations was born. With largely American financial support it tried to establish a peaceful world order. That didn't happen. So now we belong to an organization that has largely failed to bring any consensus into the world and that is even now promoting the undermining of our position in the world. Why have we continued this farce? The answer is that politicians will never admit error; the same goes for their protégés in the bureaucracy. We see this in every useless bureaucratic organization that Congress ever created. They go on and on without let up, even when they are the problem not the solution. So it shouldn't be surprising that we continue to support the United Nations.

The major reason politicians don't admit mistakes is because these mistakes were created in the first place to give our elitists a place to stand, a stage as it were, for them to promulgate law and receive their applause. It doesn't matter if what they have created just doesn't work, such as the Department of Education, the Federal Aviation Administration, the Department of Agriculture, the Department of the Interior, the Bureau of Indian Affairs, the Food and Drug Administration, and the Department of Homeland Security. No matter how expensive the mistake and no matter how costly to our lives, our freedoms, our peace of mind, and the lives of our children, they will not admit it was a mistake.

Of course, the most preeminent stage you can get is the podium at the United Nations. Here you can be the world leader, the trendsetter, the associate of power brokers, and the rich and famous. Therefore we continue to belong to and fund an organization that is not in our interests or consistent with our values. Notwithstanding this folly, we have driven our particular brand of worldview down everyone's throat who is a member nation, and we have made sure they listened by buying their attention. It doesn't matter that the values these representatives present do not in the least represent basic American values, nor does it matter that the money we pay to be heard comes from a population that does not want to be taxed for such foolishness. It only matters that they, the nation's political class, can be seen as world leaders.

By actual count we now have 282 embassies, consulates, and diplomatic missions in the world. There are 192 member states in the United Nations. Of course, many of these nations have an embassy and several consulates. There was an operations budget of $21.6 billion for this activity in 2009, which includes our expenses for the UN delegation. Of course the NSA, CIA, and all the other spy agency budgets would easily quadruple that figure if we were allow to know how much of our tax dollars was being spent on this activity. Given that we spend all this money, every year, on foreign relations and spying on foreign governments, and, don't forget, spying on our own citizens, and we still have the world we live in, what good does this do for the average American? Is it money well spent? The answer to that question depends on whether you are in the 20 percent or the 80 percent.

If the country was being run for the average middle class Americans, would we need all those embassies, consulates, missions, and spy agencies? I say no. They would ask what we were getting in return, and I think the events of 9/11 speak volumes on that subject. So why then do we continue this expense and this subjugation of our principle American values if the return for our investment is so bad? Are we afraid one man in Pakistan hiding in a cave? Does that justify this expense and this loss of our liberties? If liberty and freedom really matter to us, who is winning the War on Terror anyway? It most certainly is not us. But in truth, who is defeating us? Is it that fundamentalist Wahhabi Muslim in the cave in Pakistan or is it our own government and the way they have chosen to handle this crisis?

The point is we live in a society threatened by forces from all sides, not because we spend too much money on useless and wasteful things, but because we make no attempt to right the wrongs we do. Oops, did I say the United States of America commits wrongs? I must be a traitor.

Did you ever hear of the "herd instinct," a term coined by Sinclair Lewis in his 1922 book called "Babbit" Certainly anything written by Sinclair Lewis is worth reading; My favorite is "Kings Blood Royal", but, taps into a basic tenant of American political life that has been used by the political elite since long before Lewis's book—and ever since. He explains that you can get the majority of citizens into your herd if you just associate yourself with certain catch phrases. A Babbit is a conformist, a person in agreement with whatever you say, an emulator, follower, rubber stamper, sheep, traditionalist, the yes man, and one of the herd. So if you say, "I'm for Americanism, baseball, and apple pie," the Babbits of the world move right into your herd. I'm very sure Rush Limbaugh has read and know just how to increase his herd.

Our two political parties have been dividing us up into their particular herds for years. We now think we have a "Conservative" herd and a "Liberal" herd. Actually nothing could be farther from the truth. Most of us belong to the Manipulated herd. Political ideologues mean absolutely nothing to the herdsmen, who, as I'm sure you know by now, belong to the Political-Financial Complex that Wall Street purchases and controls. Your plebeian ideologues do not interest them in the least. They contribute to both sides and bet they will win every time. Did I mention that it is a herd of donkeys?

One of the big prizes in winning every time is the control over our foreign policy. If you can turn that big state department apparatus to promoting your businesses, then you are a real winner. But what do I mean "promoting your business"? Do I mean allowing you access to foreign markets so you can sell American-produced goods to a willing customer? Not really—that isn't the kind of access that Wall Street wants. The access they want is to be allowed to make bets in any foreign market and sell those "investments" to their clients. They want the ability to move a business in a fortnight from Kalamazoo, Michigan, to Mumbai, India, with no taxes, tariffs, or obligations; make a quick buck on the reduced labor expense; and move on. They are pushing for a seamless multinational corporate market that has no boundaries, pays no taxes, and has no laws to abide by—in short, a new world order controlled by multinational corporations that have no moral, ethical, legal, political, or economic restraints. With the help of the American government, they are almost there.

When we speak of foreign policy, there is no way around a phenomena in world politics that has existed for over sixty years and is not understood by even 10 percent of the American Middle Class, but it directly affects everything what has happened to them in those years. I'm talking about Israel. This may be the oddest foreign policy arrangement in the history of the entire world. America says that Israel is our ally, but Israeli soldiers are not fighting with us in Iraq or Afghanistan; they did not fight in the first or second Gulf wars. When they fought their wars against the Arabs—the Six-Day War, the Yom Kippur war, the Lebanon Invasion, no American soldiers were standing beside them. Yet in the recent revolts of the suppressed Arab masses in all the countries of North Africa and the Middle East against their puppet dictators, the first question asked by the American corporate news media wasn't, "What will America do?" but "How does this effect Israel?" Last I looked we only had fifty states, not fifty-one.

How did we get into this mess, and more importantly why do we continue to in this mess? As might be expected, it is complicated, and as with any U.S. foreign policy decision since the Second World War, it is completely nonsensical. Certainly the idea that the Jews of this world are from the land we have recently called Palestine cannot be denied; we have this massive book called the Bible that is the history of that people in that land. But almost from the very point that that book ends in 60 AD to the year 1917, a Jewish presence in Palestine was almost nonexistent, certainly less than 10 percent of the population. The historical term for this fact is called the Diaspora, and it is well documented. So what happened in 1917 to change this two-thousand-year separation?

The British General Edmund Allenby took the whole of Palestine away from the Turks in the First World War. Having taken it near the end of the war and effectively driving the Turks (Ottoman Empire) from the whole of Arabia, the British planned to just add it to their empire (British Commonwealth), but there was a matter that really had to be resolved, and resolved quickly, or they would find themselves in financial ruin. That was the cost of fighting the First World War. In fact both the British and the French were in the same boat, so to speak. They had insisted on making the defeated Germans pay reparations—against the advice of their American allies—because they needed the money so badly, but that only made the conditions ripe for the rise of Adolph Hitler and the Second World War. Besides, the Germans had no money to give. A solution was offered by an Austrian banking concern called the House of Rothschild. This was a European family of German Jewish origin that established European banking and finance houses from the late eighteenth century. Five lines of the Austrian branch of the family were elevated into the Austrian nobility, being given hereditary baronies of the Habsburg Empire by Emperor Francis II in 1816. The British branch of the family was elevated into the British nobility at the request of Queen Victoria. It has been argued that during the nineteenth century, the family possessed the largest private fortune in the world, and the largest fortune in modern history, by far. The British and French took the deal, and the result was the Belfour Declaration. In 1917 Walter Rothschild was the addressee of the Balfour Declaration to the Zionist Federation, which committed the British government to the establishment in Palestine of a national home for the Jewish people.

The effort began immediately to try and populate the land of Palestine with Jewish immigrants, at first it was slow going, mostly because the Jews in Europe had a very secure place and didn't want to immigrate to a desert land like Palestine. There was another serious reason not to want to go: the local population of Arabs didn't want them. But, of course, all that changed in the 1940s with the Holocaust and the strongly felt need for a Jewish homeland.

After having gone through the Holocaust, nearly all Jews were convinced they needed a homeland. Who could blame them? So a mass migration of European Jews to Palestine created conditions that had been brewing for decades and led to civil war. This is a very nasty civil war; the immigrants created a terrorist organization known as the Irgun to force the Palestinians to flee their homes so the Jews could claim them as Israeli territory. The British government tried to play the peacekeeper role, but was outflanked both politically and economically by their obligations to the Rothschild's and by the public sentiment in much of the Western world that the Jews deserved a national homeland.

There are a couple of generally accepted processes that sensible people would expect from a conquering nation when they take over a populated area not previously belonging to them. They are (1) look for a way to resolve differences, (2) seek to assimilate the defeated population into your new political and economic structure, (3) allow them to continue to worship their deity as they believe, and (4) if you have taken private property, justly compensate them for their loss. Failing to do these things will not pacify the indigenous population and will certainly make you look like a barbarian to the rest of humanity.

In 1947 the Jewish state was proclaimed in Palestine, and who was the first to recognize them? The United States! If you had been around at that time, you would have been astounded. Logically, one would have expected the first to be Britain or France, not America. Why? Well for one, no one thought we really had any interest in that part of the world, as did Britain and France, who were maintaining colonial empires at the time, and two, the issue of a Jewish homeland was still in very hot debate here from both a political and a social point of view.

This is where the fog of history gets very, very thick and, in fact, has never dissipated, leaving us with a heap of conspiracy theories that are constantly being revised and seem to reproduce of their own power, they are that prolific. It is often pointed out that the Jewish community in America was a very big supporter of this new Jewish state, and even though their numbers did not come close to a huge voting bloc, they did possess one important lever: they controlled a large percentage of the news media in the United States. Another theory is that this Jewish influence came to prominence because they were traditional Democrats and Harry Truman was in the fight of his life to defeat Dewey, the Republican candidate, in 1948—and their contributions to his campaign fund put him over the top. While both of these statements are true, they do not constitute a conspiracy. A conspiracy is not something you do in public for all to see; it is something you do in private where it is kept secret.

Whatever the motives, the deal was struck. We had a new best friend, Israel. The problem is that they still have this PR problem from the way they took over Palestine and the way they administered it afterward. If you take land by conquest or you just steal it, the way to avoid a continuous problem is to pay for it. But ever since the state of Israel was created, it has refused to pay reparations. Now I'm not going to suggest that reparations will solve this problem— it won't. Many, many issues need to be addressed before this problem is going to be solved, but the resolution of this problem does have at least a cost verses results quotient that should be considered.

The resolution of this problem is essential for America because our politicians say it is, not because it makes any difference to the American Middle Class who controls Palestine, it absolutely does not. There is nothing strategic about Palestine: they have no oil, they have no rare minerals, they are no breadbasket of the world; there is not one reason for us to care. But ever since 1947 we have cared, and it has become the cornerstone of our foreign policy— the most costly cornerstone ever laid. We pay Israel about $32 billion every year, in one form or another. What we get for that payment isn't much worth having; we get the eternal enmity of every Arab and Muslim nation. We get constant warfare with them, higher prices for almost everything they produce, and the status of hypocrites in the eyes of the world—and in our own eyes. We are literally forcing a theocracy upon a subjugated people who have no say in their government or in their future. All other Arab states have frozen immigration from Palestine to keep the fires burning, so the resident population can't even escape legally. Now this book is about American values and how we have lost them; could there be a better example of that then this foreign policy imperative the Democrats and Republicans have forced on all of us? I would be remiss if I didn't also give credit to the Jewish lobby in Washington, the corporate media they control, and the millions they spend to keep this ridiculous policy. There is something disturbing about people who immigrate to this country but use all their wealth and influence to support another country to the detriment of our own. After all, this is the country who nourished them, educated them, gave them opportunity, and kept them from the hands of the corrupt and ruthless governments whence they escaped. But instead of grati tude and fraternity, they give this country unending misery and division for the sake of a country they wouldn't even live in. If you have no regard for the community that nourished you, what kind of a person are you? If you come here to establish your own community and not join ours, why would we call you an American or ever give you citizenship?

"If you want to make peace, you don't talk to your friends, you talk to your enemies." —Moshe Dayan

How many people know the real situation? Perhaps I should rephrase that: how many Americans know the real situation? The world knows the truth; Americans don't. The corporate news simply will not mention this. Political parties will not even defend this foreign policy because for anyone to question it is simply un-American. Why is that? We have a foreign policy cornerstone that has made us enemies in fully half of the world and hypocrites in the rest of the world, and we are not even allowed to question it, lest we be un-American? Did you never wonder why political correctness is really a problem for those of us who believe in the First Amendment? The French are said to have an axiom when it comes to solving crime, "Cher chi le femme", find the women. In America we have an axiom for solving crime: "Follow the money trail." If you want the why's behind our foreign policy, the procedure is the same.

Maybe the biggest question is why do we have a foreign policy so focused on Europe, Asia, and the Middle East when our country doesn't border any of these places? Our real concerns and our real future are in this hemisphere, the area of North and South America. We have a tidal wave of immigration flooding us from the south. We have drug lords who have taken over whole provinces in Mexico and other areas south of our border. We are witnessing wholesale corruption to our south, yet we have fixed our gaze to the east and the west and never look elsewhere. We have an eye disease: we have no peripheral vision.

Unfortunately, the Palestine–Israel question is just the tip of the iceberg when it comes to our foreign policy. If you asked yourself what policy decisions would most hurt the American people, strain our relationships with everyone else on this planet, and destroy any credibility we ever had as a freedom-loving nation, you would decide to follow the present foreign policy of the United States. It makes no sense; it hasn't made sense in the lifetimes of anyone reading this book, no matter how old you are. It will never make any sense in the future if we continue in the footsteps of our current leadership. It appears to purposely go against every reasonable interest we have in this world.

Why are we not supporting our neighbors to the south: Mexico, Guatemala, El Salvatore, Nicaragua, Honduras, and Costa Rica, with help to establish democratic governments, provide economic equality for their people, quash corruption in their justice system, and improve the lot of their citizens? If you don't know the answer to this one, you simply haven't absorbed anything I've been saying. The Republican and Democratic Parties have denied exactly these same things to 80 percent of American citizens, so why would you think they are going to try and encourage it in our neighbors? The simple truth is that we are not who we say we are, and so long as these two parties rule, it will remain that way.

"No nation can preserve its freedom in the midst of continual warfare" — James Madison – Political Observations 1795

HOW DO WE FIX THIS?

America is the pawn of multinational corporations: our foreign policy has no relationship to the security and prosperity of our people and has only to do with what Wall Street and the multinational corporations like Shell, British Petroleum, and Halliburton (a Dubai corporation) want. We did not attack Iraq to save Israel, as the Islamic nations believe; we attacked them to save the oil for the big oil companies and to protect our enemy—Saudi Arabia. We attacked Afghanistan as a substitute for Saudi Arabia to placate the American people after 9/11. We support ruthless dictators and we maintain friendly relations with monarchies and theocracies, forms of government in direct opposition with our own, because Wall Street and the multinational corporations want it that way.

We do support Israel against all reason for objectives that have never been explained or even declared to the American Middle Class. If we support Israel because we are being blackmailed and bribed to do so, I think we citizens should know that. If we are supporting Israel because the pro-Israeli lobby controls the news media, I think we citizens should know that. If we support Israel because groups of Christian fundamentalist believe we should from their interpretation of the Bible, I think we citizens should know that. Bottom line we citizens are owed an explanation in clear and uncertain terms as to why the cornerstone of our foreign policy exists.

Our foreign policy has nothing to do with what is right or what will help our citizens. If we had a foreign policy designed to protect American citizens and create real stability in the world, we would drop all support for any dictatorial or nondemocratic society, just as our Founders advised. We would attack and destroy our real enemies, the Saudis, and we would be sure to kill every Wahhabi we can find; they attacked us on 9/11—remember? We would stop all stupid wars of aggression, bring our troops home from every corner of the world, and let it be known we stand for peace not war.

Against the insidious wiles of foreign influence (I conjure you to believe me, fellow-citizens), the jealousy of a free people ought to be constantly awake; since history and experience prove that foreign influence is one of the most baneful foes of republican government. But that jealousy, to be useful, must be impartial; else it becomes the instrument of the very influence to be avoided, instead of

a defence against it. Excessive partiality for one foreign nation, and excessive dislike of another, cause those whom they actuate to see danger only on one side, and serve to veil and even second the arts of influence on the other. Real Patriots, who may resist the intrigues of the favorite, are liable to become suspected and odious; while its tools and dupes usurp the applause and confidence of the people, to surrender their interests. - George Washington in his farewell address September 1796

The citizens of this republic need to remind themselves that every war we engage in and every dictator we send hard-earned money to—billions every year for each one of them—is money taken from our Social Security fund, forcing us to retire at seventy instead of sixty-five, from our paychecks in the form of ever higher taxes, from our profits because we can't sell our goods to people who hate us, from our children's education and our freedom because we are always having to "protect" ourselves from the enemies we make with money and restrictions. There is a real cost to this foreign policy and we are paying it.

These chapters have been pretty heavy; here is a historical bit of humor from a Founder – Ben Franklin.

"George Washington, Commander of the American armies, who like Joshua of old, commanded the sun and the moon to stand still, and they obeyed him." —From Benjamin Franklin's toast at a dinner of foreign dignitaries at Versailles, after the British foreign minister toasted King George III, likening him to the sun, and the French minister toasted Louis XVI, likening him to the moon, 1781.

Chapter 7
Education: Academia

"**B**ut of all the views of this law none is more important, none more legitimate, than that of rendering the people the safe, as they are the ultimate, guardians of their own liberty. For this purpose the reading in the first stage, where they will receive their whole education, is proposed, as has been said, to be chiefly historical. History by apprising them of the past will enable them to judge of the future; it will avail them of the experience of other times and other nations; it will qualify them as judges of the actions and designs of men; it will enable them to know ambition under every disguise it may assume; and knowing it, to defeat its views." —Thomas Jefferson, Notes on the State of Virginia, Query 14, 1781

From very early in the twentieth century until the 1970s, the United States was always in the top three nations in education according to the Organization for Education Cooperation and Development (OECD). Quite often it was number one. Since the 1970s the country's standing has been in slow decline. In 2007, this United States didn't even make it into the top thirty, something that has been a major campaign issue for politicians, a big factor in where parents choose to live, and a source of huge amounts of money for many state governments, supposed nonprofit organizations, and corporations. Almost unanimously everyone calls out for more tax dollars and more emphasis on education, but is this the answer? Money and emphasis have not resolved this problem in the past thirty years. Education suffers from too much money ill spent, too much attention, and way too much politics. For starters, I will give you one fact to muse over. The current Department of Education was established in 1979 to ensure more uniformity among the state education systems, improved instruction in math and science, and higher graduation rates for students. It was a centerpiece of the Carter administration. It has failed on every count. The states that trailed in education in 1980 are still at the bottom. The USA still lags behind other industrialized nations in math and science. Graduation rates are lower now than they were in 1980. Nevertheless, politicians, parents, the National Education Association (NEA) and other nonprofits, and state educators are all much better at statistics and the manipulation of them. There is more money spent on education now than in 1980 but far less reaches the classrooms. How do we really improve education in this country? Well, first we need to get all the people who know absolutely nothing about education out of the picture, especially politicians.

Before we dive into the details of how to improve education, I want to bring to your attention an underlying problem to muse on as you read. In our media-driven culture, the people being celebrated are seldom intellectual achievers. We as a nation don't respect intelligence and wisdom like we do artistic ability, good looks, and the ability to make money in any fashion. *Of course* our youth don't value it either. In the past five years, several young women have become celebrities, asked to star in movies, or given their own TV reality show, thus becoming wealthy, by first making a lurid sex tape of themselves and putting it on the internet for all to see. And every time adults watch these films or TV shows, they are educating their children to believe this is how to live. Good job, parents. Yes, we need to establish are middle class values again in education too.

Since 1979 the percentage of education dollars going to administrative costs and not to the classroom has gone up by a factor of 90 percent. That is money the children don't get. That is money the taxpayer is being cheated out of. It is money for the legion of morons who back the political candidate but know nothing about education. Of course, they still make education policy. Let's take a look at the 2011 education budget as compiled by Christopher Chantrill for "US Government Spending." Note that numbers are in the billions of dollars.

Table 7: Total education spending by levels of government in the U.S.

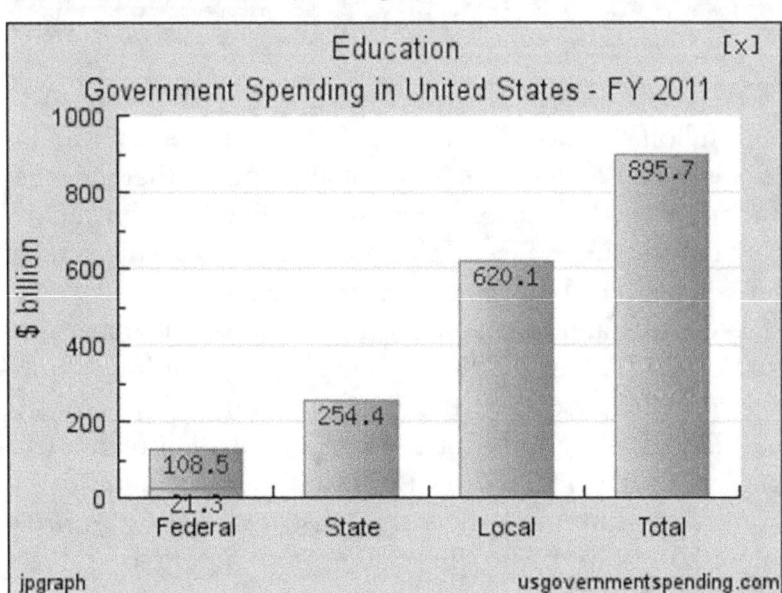

So now let's see what it looks like for the K–12 kids:

Table 8: K-12 education spending by levels of government in the U.S.

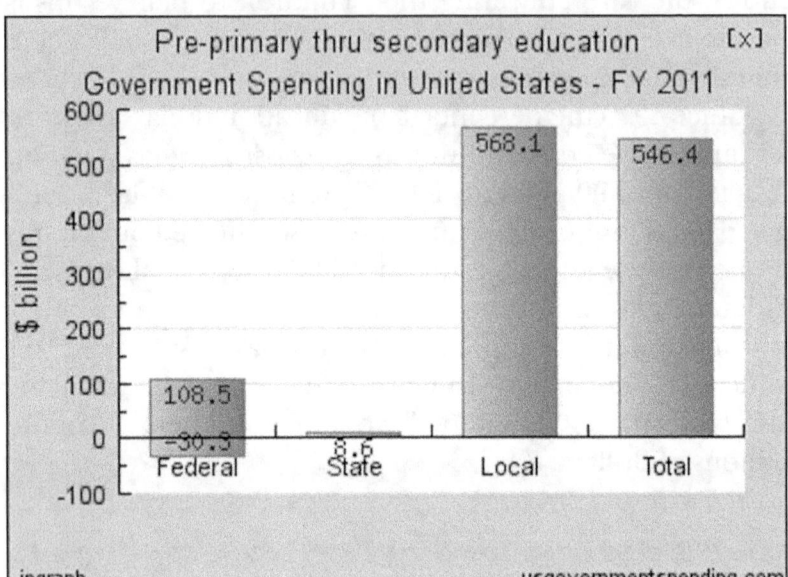

Actually the federal government is spending about $30 billion dollars as a deficit in 2011 for education. But when it comes to K–12 education, note, dear taxpayer, that the local budget exceeds state and federal spending by an incalculable amount since they don't do deficit spend. That total is actually higher than the combined total.

Now it is almost axiomatic to ask, how is it that if the entire real budget for K–12 educational spending is coming from local sources the federal government thinks it should be calling the shots on curriculum? Unfortunately, that isn't the worse part of these statistics; the administrative cost of running your school district is almost entirely due to responding to that same Department of Education in Washington, D.C. So your school district is forced to hire administrators, accountants, and lawyers to keep the demanding bureaucrats happy. All that money and all that effort are spent in deference to the children being educated. Next we might ask, if the local district is paying for the whole thing, why are they spending so much time answering to the federal government? Does the question not yet sound familiar? Because they are the Elite, because they know more than you, because they have law degrees, not degrees in education? By now I'm sure all of that makes sense to you. I think not!

So we have a system where the federal government tells the states what curriculum they have to emphasize and the states tell the local districts what they have to do to meet the federal criteria. The federal and state governments build up large bureaucracies, which forces the local districts to build a bureaucracy to deal with the other levels. All that structure is expensive, and it is focused on a political agenda, not on what it takes to educate a child. Do you see anything wrong with this system?

The federal political agenda is that we should produce more math and science majors, so that is the goal. There is no inquiry into how many children are interested in math and science, just a mandate and a rating system to go with the mandate as to how well each district is meeting the quota. Of course, this being a federal mandate, it is unfunded, but the quota system sounds rather like a "Five Year Plan" famously created by our Russian and Chinese Communist friends, wouldn't you say? You know, where the state says it is going to run everything, right down to what your children aspire to be. I don't know about you, but that just doesn't feel like an American value. Actually it doesn't sound anything like the freedoms and liberties our Founding Fathers had in mind. But I'm sure you haven't forgot, that old idea of having a Declaration of Independence and a Constitution that was actually the highest law of the land is really out of fashion isn't it? Our progressive-revisionist friends have ditched that idea a long time ago, and just look at how much the American Middle Class has benefitted from their brilliant insights.

The kindergartener in Head Start and the high school student in Title 1 Entitlement programs all have their highly advanced education due to the intervention of the federal government, which doesn't pay for anything really but assures a uniform standard of excellence throughout the school system. Just one thing wrong with that: America is slipping further and further every year in the ranking of nations' educational systems. Could it be that the premise is wrong?

I think educating our children to a politically driven agenda is the wrong premise. It is a formula for mediocrity. Most children gravitate toward their life interests as they become exposed to them. It's not something that politicians, teachers, or even parents can decide for them. This is not to say that parents and teachers don't make the decisions—actually it happens more often than not, but to accomplish the successful rearing of a child you want to be observant, not dictatorial. The good teacher, the good parent, is observant, looking for that spark of enthusiasm that indicates genuine interest. Politicians have no valid role in this process and therefore must be excluded. When you get that match of a child's interest with the subject, you are certain to have real learning take place. I don't want to suggest that you cannot achieve results the other way; sitting with children and working with them on specific subjects to instill a discipline that will result in good academic performance across the board. If you do both, the results are sure to be excellent. The idea that a child bent on horse raising is somehow going to find a fulfilling life as a chemical engineer is really not practical or likely to produce anything more than a mediocre engineer.

Education really is a place where politics does not apply. It is also a place where overbearing bureaucracies are counterproductive. I think any parent who has raised more than one child knows that the one-size-fits-all idea of our public schools is absurd. As the child grows older, the problem just becomes exacerbated. The regimented models of kindergarten and elementary school learning give way to more focused and more individualized methods. Some children learn visually, some are better with the written word, and still others have an abstract way of thinking that is hard to recognize and harder still to fit into a classroom of thirty students. The diversity of opportunity available for children to learn is much more important than any national political agenda for their learning.

I think most parents know by observation that the best schools have the best principals. It is the principal who sets the tone in a school. This is where we need to focus. We don't need school district superintendents making $150,000 to over $200,000 to get good schools. We need a very specific focus on principals. We need to empower them, remove the legislated burdens from them, and then follow up regularly to see how they are managing.

If we do these things, we won't be looking at charts like the one below in the future.

Table 9: Top 30 countries for Pisa 2009 results in Math, Sciences, and Reading.

Programme for International Student Assessment (2009)
(OECD members as of the time of the study in boldface)

Maths		Sciences		Reading	
1. Shanghai, China	600	1. Shanghai, China	575	1. Shanghai, China	556
2. Singapore	562	2. **Finland**	554	2. **South Korea**	539
3. Hong Kong, China	555	3. Hong Kong, China	549	3. **Finland**	536
4. **South Korea**	546	4. Singapore	542	4. Hong Kong, China	533
5 Taiwan	543	5. **Japan**	539	5. Singapore	526
6. **Finland**	541	6. **South Korea**	538	6. **Canada**	524
7. Liechtenstein	536	7. **New Zealand**	532	7. **New Zealand**	521
8. **Switzerland**	534	8. **Canada**	529	8. **Japan**	520
9. **Japan**	529	9. Estonia	528	9. **Australia**	515
10. **Canada**	527	10. **Australia**	527	10. **Netherlands**	508
11. **Netherlands**	526	11. **Netherlands**	522	11. **Belgium**	506

12. Macau, China 525	12. Liechtenstein 520	12. **Norway** 503
13. **New Zealand** 519	13. **Germany** 520	13. Estonia 501
14. **Belgium** 515	14. Taiwan 520	14. **Switzerland** 501
15. **Australia** 514	15. **Switzerland** 517	15. **Poland** 500
16. **Germany** 513	16. **United Kingdom** 514	16. **Iceland** 500
17. Estonia 512	7. Slovenia 512	17. **United States** 500
18. **Iceland** 507	18. Macau, China 511	18. Liechtenstein 499
19. **Denmark** 503	19. **Poland** 508	19. **Sweden** 497
20. Slovenia 501	20. **Ireland** 508	20. **Germany** 497
21. **Norway** 498	21. **Belgium** 507	21. **Ireland** 496
22. **France** 497	22. **Hungary** 503	22. **France** 496
23. **Slovakia** 497	23. **United States** 502	23. Taiwan 495
24. **Austria** 496	24. **Norway** 500	24. **Denmark** 495

25. Poland	495	25. Czech Republic	500	25. United Kingdom	494
26. Sweden	494	26. Denmark	499	26. Hungary	494
27. Czech Republic	493	27. France	498	27. Portugal	489
28. United Kingdom	492	28. Iceland	496	28. Macau, China	487
29. Hungary	490	29. Sweden	495	29. Italy	486
30. United States	487	30. Latvia	494	30. Latvia	484
65. Kyrgyzstan	331	65. Kyrgyzstan	330	65 Kyrgyzstan	314

It can be said that all the Founding Fathers were very interested in education, but the one that stands out is Thomas Jefferson. The education of the common man had occupied his thoughts for decades. He believed ignorance to be the enemy of freedom, and he wanted to correct what he considered to be the defects of educational institutions modeled on European settings and curriculum. He imagined that an "academical village" clustered around a tree-lined lawn would provide an ideal setting in which to pursue higher education. The focal point of such a village would be a Temple of Knowledge that would house the university library.

When the Virginia legislature authorized a state university in 1818, the retired U.S. president finally was able to dedicate his intellect, time, and energy to creating this new kind of educational institution. By the time he was finished with his design, Jefferson had invented a uniquely American setting for higher education: the college campus. Jefferson's early experiences and observations about education led him to conclude that the practice of housing students, faculty, classrooms, and dining halls in a single large building was not a satisfactory arrangement. While serving as president, Jefferson wrote a letter to Littleton Tazewell, one of the delegates to the Virginia legislature, offering his observations on a proposal to create a new state university:

"The greatest danger will be their overbuilding themselves by attempting a large house in the beginning, sufficient to contain the whole institution. Large houses are always ugly, inconvenient, exposed to accident of fire, and in bad cases of infection. A plain small house for the school & lodging of each professor is best. These connected by covered ways out of which the rooms of the students should open would be best. These may then be built as they shall be wanting. In fact, a University should not be a house but a village. This will much lessen their first expenses."

After retiring from the presidency, Jefferson's thoughts about an ideal university were taking clear shape, even though Virginia's state representatives had not yet passed legislation to create a system of public education:

No one more sincerely wishes the spread of information among mankind than I do, and none has greater confidence in its effect towards supporting free and good government. I, am sincerely rejoiced, therefore, to find that so excellent a fund has been provided for this noble purpose in Tennessee.... I consider the common plan [for colleges]

165

followed in this country, but not in others, of making one large and expensive building, as unfortunately erroneous. It is infinitely better to erect a small and separate lodge for each professorship, with only a hall below for his class and two chambers above for himself; joining these lodges by barracks for a certain portion of the students, opening into a covered way to give a dry communication between all the schools. The whole of these arranged around an open square of grass and trees would make it what it should be in fact, an academical village.... Much observation and reflection on these institutions have long convinced me that the large and crowded buildings in which youths are pent up are equally unfriendly to health, to study, to manners, morals, and order.

Once the law establishing the university was enacted, Thomas Jefferson personally transformed his ideas into reality. He applied his remarkable intellect to design a university whose physical presence and course of studies would produce an educated citizenry capable of defending the freedom and democracy of the new United States of America. Jefferson produced beautiful neoclassical plans, including those for the five pavilions to house faculty and students, which he designed in an astonishing fifteen days. He enthusiastically described his plans to mathematician Nathaniel Bowditch in his letter of October 26, 1818:

The legislature passed an act establishing a university, endowing it for the present with an annuity of fifteen thousand dollars and directing commissioners to meet to recommend a site, a plan of buildings... The plan of building is not to erect one single magnificent building to contain everybody and everything, but to make of it an academical village in which every professor should have his separate house [called 'pavilions'], containing his lecturing room with two, three, or four rooms for his own accommodation according as he may have a family or no family, with kitchen, garden, etc.; distinct dormitories for the students, not more than two in a room; and separate boarding houses [called hotels] for dieting them by private housekeepers. We concluded to employ no professor who is not of the first order of the science he professes, that when we can find such in our own country we shall prefer them and when we cannot we will procure them wherever else to be found.

Jefferson not only drew the architectural plans of the buildings but also made the four-mile trip between his home, Monticello, and the University on horseback almost every day to oversee construction. The elder statesman was as attentive to detail as he was to the overall concept; for example, he stipulated that the university's bronze bell have an acoustical range of two miles, and he also designed the brickyard to supply the university's construction.

Construction of the university was slow and plagued by tight budgets, religious and political opposition, and critics of the university's aesthetics. Nonetheless, by the time the university opened its doors to the first 125 students in 1825, ten pavilions had been constructed to house the first professors and their families. A colonnaded passageway bordered the east and west sides of the Lawn (the central open space), connecting the two-story pavilions with the adjacent student dormitory rooms. The south end of the Lawn was intentionally left open to views of the mountains beyond. At the head of the Lawn stood the Rotunda, an impressive domed structure, which housed the university library. This building was modeled on a famous Roman temple, the Pantheon, which had been built between 118 and 128 A.D. Two rows of secondary buildings, known as the East and West Range, were constructed parallel to the Lawn. The Range contained more student rooms interspersed with six dining halls, linked again by a covered passageway. Between the buildings of the Lawn and the Range Jefferson included gardens enclosed by serpentine brick walls that were shared by the professors and hotelkeepers (the families who ran the student dining halls). Thomas Jefferson had succeeded in taking his ideals about education and democracy, transforming them into a working plan, and producing the University of Virginia.

Now I would like you to stop a moment here and think about what you just read. Could you ever again believe that the Founders of this nation were not wholly committed to the future generations and focused on making this country the fountainhead of culture, knowledge, and civility? Don't let the misinformation campaigns circulating throughout the media misguide you; no one sits down and plans a school of higher learning that he will likely never see finished, and will certainly never be able to teach in or attend, if he is not wholly focused on future generations and what will make their lives more fulfilling. The Founding Fathers had your pursuit of happiness in mind when they wrote the Constitution, and they continued to pursue policies and programs that would ensure community bonds and opportunity for future generations.

As has been shown we must get politicians out of education; we must get unions out of education. We must get values, American values, back into education. The grand schemes of policy in both of our two parties for a global economy and a worldwide government include having the serfs prepared for the role the government will tell them to play. It doesn't have any room for the role the individual wants to play. If we continue to allow Washington to dictate what our children will and will not learn, we are only hurrying the day they can all become cogs in the great wheel the elite have been planning for the past fifty years. I have two grandchildren they are very unique individuals and I would hate to see them waste their time here doing the things the elite think are important and not the things they were born to do. I know their happiness depends on what we do now to stop this nonsense.

We can't leave the subject of education without discussing the challenge that getting a college education has become in this country. Our nation has developed a widespread and effective higher educational system. The private institutions notwithstanding, we have a system of land grant universities and colleges that have been second to none, and they exist in every state of the union. In recent times, however, two very serious problems have developed that threaten to undo all that was accomplished. The first is the increase in cost of getting a higher education. We have made this cost so high that we now automatically exclude 80 percent of the population from getting a higher education. If you are in the 80 percent that lives on just 15 percent of the nation's wealth, going to college is a goal that has slipped away from you. You can get student loans backed by the government through Sallie Mae, but this is a sucker's bet: if you take one of these loans, you will incur a debt that could last you for the rest of your life. You may never actually get that degree you started out to get, but you will never get rid of your debt. Your two devoted political parties have exempted student loans from bankruptcy actions, so no matter what you do or what may happen, you will have to pay it back in full—sick, unemployed, living on the street, mentally disabled—doesn't matter, you are stuck. Do not take out a student loan—it is a very bad deal that has been arranged for you by our good friends on Wall Street, who lobbied the Bush administration to change the bankruptcy laws so they could get every last dime you ever owed them regardless of your circumstances. President Bush signed it into law. Student loans have joined credit cards as a devise that you should never sign up for, lest you enter into economic slavery for all of your life.

The second issue is the quality of that education. In times past we had undergraduate classes taught by full professors at these excellent institutions; today undergraduate students are lucky if they ever see a full professor in the entire four years of their sojourn at college. Classes are now taught by graduate students, who have no real world experience and no credentials to be teaching your child. Somehow that is considered acceptable even though you are paying much, much more for the education than was ever required in the past. This has consequences: we now are seeking to bring in people with needed degrees from all over the world for the jobs our own graduates used to fill, but no longer can. They have the sheepskin and the enormous debt, but they really didn't get an education. It seems no one in academia cares about that; just send them to graduate school and we'll have real professors teach them. Too bad they're too far in debt to afford to go to graduate school.

HOW DO WE FIX THIS?

I guess by now no one is surprised that yet another cherished institution of the American past has succumbed to the prevailing paradigm of greed, power, and globalization, but this time it really hits home: it's our children, damn it. I'm sure you know that voting for either political party will only maintain the status quo, which isn't in the interest of our children or the American Middle Class. So when we stop voting for these jackasses, we need to formulate political entities, either grassroots movements or middle class funded political parties that are determined to take politics out of the classroom.

The very first thing is to eliminate the Department of Education. That alone will make your wallet sigh with relief. Then we must bring education back to the children. I am very sympathetic to the teachers out there now doing all they can to teach our children amidst this political fiasco we have created, but even for them, I would not lift a finger until we have refocused education back to the whole point of doing it—the children. We cannot continue to treat them like they were some asset of the state and the state's ambitions to dominate the new world order, like the first President Bush loved to promote.

Education is for the children. Get the politicians and bureaucrats out of it. Put all your dollars on the classroom, not the administration. Get rid of every high-salaried administrator. We need a Constitutional amendment to say that the U.S. Congress and the president have absolutely no power to interfere in our educational system, and if they try, impeachment will follow. Then we need to look at all that money we saved by kicking the Washington gang out and start offering real incentives to teachers, with really good salaries for the proven ones. We also need to make sure we have university training in being a school administrator for those who, after having proven their abilities as teachers, are then asked to move to the principal's office. This would be a graduate degree with tuition, room, and board paid by the local school district. Believe me, you will never spend your money more wisely than when you ensure you have good principles in your schools. We need to separate boys and girls in the middle school years. Each gender needs that separation to define themselves and establish their identity separate from their need to fit in. This will produce a healthier individual both physically and mentally.

It isn't enough to stop there: we have to have follow-up. If a school starts to slip in the quality of its education, we need to step in immediately and make changes. Similarly, we need to correct the direction our universities and colleges are headed. I'm talking about the state-funded land grant institutions—private schools can go in whatever direction they want. But for the taxpayer supported institutions we have to stop hiring PR people as the university presidents and hire real educators. We need to quit making the athletics program the major factor in the measure of school success and start counting our academic achievements, How many Rhodes Scholars do we have; how many Nobel Lariats have we produced? Is our school known for its community outreach? Do our professors visit the towns and cities in our state and talk to the elementary and high school students there? Are we just sending graduate students to these functions? If your professors aren't teaching and aren't involved in community outreach, why then are we paying their salaries? Move them out and let's get people dedicated to being educators not grant writers.

Chapter 8
Science

"In the spring of 1760, [I] went to William and Mary college, where I continued two years. It was my great good fortune, and what probably fixed the destinies of my life, that Dr. William Small of Scotland, was then Professor of Mathematics, a man profound in most of the useful branches of science, with a happy talent of communication, correct and gentlemanly manners, and an enlarged and liberal mind. He, most happily for me, became soon attached to me, and made me his daily companion when not engaged in the school; and from his conversation I got my first views of the expansion of science, and of the system of things in which we are placed." —Thomas Jefferson

Let me just start out by saying whenever anyone speaking about science says that the debate is over, the issue is settled, then they are by definition no longer talking about science. The end of science is when debate stops. At that point you have demagoguery.

Politicians are very used to demagoguery—they swim in it—but scientists who insist that the debate is over are forfeiting their credentials and abandoning their profession. Personally, I would much prefer to be a scientist than a politician. I think these scientists have made a very poor choice.

Of course, I'm referring to the ongoing controversy over climate change. At first the promoters of the human-caused source (anthropogenic) of climate change made it axiomatic that if you challenged them you didn't believe that climate change was going on at all. However, few scientists would doubt that climate change is taking place; this was just a ploy to stop investigation and discussion of the causes. You see, it had become financially rewarding to be a proponent of the idea that humans caused the climate to change. Big government grants were available for you and your institution if you joined their side. You as a scientist would receive a lot of institutional pressure to go along with the flow and follow the money. After all, the European Union was promoting the anthropogenic origins of climate change, and they were doing everything in their power to get the rest of the world to agree with them. Money was no object. Unfortunately, most of the world *did* go along with this political push to declare open season on any scientist who objected to the hasty conclusions. So the money flowed and the papers "proving" that climate change was caused by human activity, i.e., CO_2, piled up.

What if CO_2 isn't the only cause? What if there are other known causes that aren't in vogue? What if CO_2 isn't even the *leading* cause of climate change? Why would the European Union want so desperately to shut off scientific debate that they would use their entire political apparatus to do it? What possible reason would they have to want the cause to be human caused? Does the phrase "carbon credits" mean anything to you? Who in the world could really profit from the trading of carbon credits? Who is best positioned to make the most of these credits? Would it be the governments of Europe and, for that matter, any highly industrialized sector of the world economy? Was there ever anything as transparent as this grab for billions of free tax dollars flowing to the industrial countries from the startup, newly industrializing countries?

Still wonder why the push to make global warming a solely human caused source?

"Reason and free inquiry are the only effectual agents against error." —Thomas Jefferson

The politicization of science is one of the greatest disservices to humanity in our lifetimes. We must recognize that technological societies rely on the integrity and openness of science. To reduce science to demagoguery is a crime. If our accreditation institutions had any real principles, they would take action to remove from their membership those who espoused closing off debate on any scientific investigation. Anyone over forty knows that at least two-thirds of our gross national product (GNP) is generated from the scientific advances we made during the time we were competing with the Russians in our race to the moon. The jobs that the space race generated by creating new competitive technology account for *all* of our economic growth in the past forty years. So we citizens have a real stake in what the government does with our tax dollars to invest in the future of technology. Short-sighted and wrong-headed goals will certainly make us poorer and will likely mean that our children don't have jobs.

Now make no mistake about were I'm coming from: there is definitely climate change going on. However, the tragedy is that we really don't know enough to determine whether it will be detrimental or to our advantage. The main reason for that is the fact that we no longer fund any alternative ideas about what is causing climate change. This was seen at the time of the Copenhagen meeting when it was revealed how the British Climate Change Institute was attempting to falsify temperature data and influence peer-review boards all over the world, even to the point of trying to get people who asked challenging questions thrown off these review boards. Why? Because these institutions want to keep the grant and research funds flowing to them.

The price we are paying for this is more than we or our children will ever be able to bear. Our sun was behaving in a most extraordinary way in the late 1990s and early 2000s. We have never witnessed anything like it since Galileo invented the telescope over four hundred years ago. It was measured to be 55 percent hotter than what was thought to be normal and was spitting out solar flares on a frequent basis that exceeded the scales we had made to measure them. Those highly charged particles were bombarding us with very high rem (coulomb) rates in the X-ray range, and they were impacting our upper atmosphere by creating large numbers of free radicals that then interacted with the nitrogen and oxygen in our atmosphere. That interaction then created clouds of nitric oxides, a greenhouse gas that was measured to be thousand times greater than the volume of CO^2, our old friend, in the atmosphere. Any of that sound anthropogenic to you?

The question of the impact of greenhouse gases has been around for quite some time now. It is a subject of considerable debate in scientific circles. Much of that debate goes unnoticed by the general public because it is really not news worthy or something they need to navigate through their lives. But when a person who has the public spotlight enters the debate it changes the landscape and raises the need for the public to understand the core elements of that debate. This happened when Al Gore began promoting the anthropogenic base for climate change. His time phased charts and accomplished public speaking talents convinced many people that a real danger was present and could be avoid if we changed our ways.

Before Mr. Gore entered the fray a very serious and extended debate was going on among scientist which concern an epoch period in earth history before the advent of the human species. That debate concerned the Miocene epoch period and it extends from about 23.03 to 5.32 million years ago (Ma). During this Miocene period average temperatures on earth were warmer than they are now by about 3 degrees Kelvin (3 degrees Celsius) or 5.4 degrees Fahrenheit. That is actually a significant change if you consider that in the last 80 years the average temperature on earth has only gone up by about 0.6 degrees Celsius. Yet with this we have seen the hottest temperatures ever recorded in many areas of the world. So a 3 degree rise in the average temperature is significant. I'm sure I don't have to point out to you that there were no human beings existing on earth at this time, yet we see a significant rise in temperatures; enough to melt the poles, raise the sea level, and turn prairies into deserts. The scientific question was what were the agents that caused this rise in temperature, if one assumes that the CO_2 level was equal to pre-industrialized earth then what drove the temperature up in the Miocene age? Another consideration is that we know from ice core samples that we see a rise in CO_2 levels on average about every 12,000 years, what causes that? We are very sure it's not anthropogenic, but really want to understand the drivers in these changes. Could these same non CO_2 causes be what is driving our current climate change?

The trouble with spending all scientific funds for research on politically driven agendas is that we lose the opportunity to find out what is really happening and we lose scientific objectivity. As with religion, science and politics just do not mix. Maybe the most overlooked and probably the most significant factor in the causes of our changing climate is the movement of the northern and southern magnetic poles. Earth has two geographic poles: the North Pole and the South Pole. They are the places on Earth's surface that Earth's imaginary axis passes through. Our planet also has two magnetic poles: the North Magnetic Pole (NMP) and the South Magnetic Pole (SMP). The magnetic poles are near, but not quite in the same places as, the geographic poles. The needle in a compass points toward a magnetic pole. Earth's magnetic poles are actually pretty far from its geographic poles. In 2005, the North Magnetic Pole (NMP) was about 810 km (503 miles) from the geographic North Pole and as recently as 2010 was measured to be moving at 72 km per year due north, it could cross the Arctic sea and move into Siberia sometime in the next century. Remember it has been in northern Canada for all of our lifetimes. The NMP was in the Arctic Ocean north of Canada. The SMP was about 2,826 km (1,756 miles) from the geographic South Pole, off the coast of Antarctic in the direction of Australia. During the Amundsen–Scott race to the South Pole in 1910–1912, Roald Amundsen, a world-renowned Norwegian scientist and polar explorer even before this expedition, found and measured the South Pole to be near the middle of the Antarctic continent. The magnetic field of Earth, influenced by the strength of the solar wind, determines the movement of the jet streams, which in turn control our climate. Doesn't it just make sense that its movement by 1756 miles might proscribe some sort of change in our climate? Yet humans did not cause this.

History records many periods when science, usually without any political help, managed to derail itself and produce little of importance. The late nineteenth century was a time like that. It was finally broken by Einstein's 1905 paper on relativity. More recently, we have seen a twenty-five-year drought caused by the takeover of nearly all of the nations' physics departments by a group dedicated to string theory.

If you want tenure or if you just wanted to be hired, you had better say you believe in string theory. The problem is that string theory produces nothing, and it can't even make a valid prediction of anything. It is, however, beautiful mathematics. We await the next Einstein.

I mention this to point out that following the crowd is not always in the best interests of those who join the herd. Recent examples are the topic of acid rain—proven by more than three thousand scientists working all over the world to be caused by volcanic action, not human action, the media pundits notwithstanding. The Y2K panic was caused by misinformed media more than anything else. Actually it might be more correct to say media unwilling to debunk an obvious overstatement by a few academic "scientist' who didn't know what they were talking about. And now we can add to the list the CO^2 scare of the early twenty-first century. The difference is this one will have a heavier and longer-lasting impact than the other two combined.

"I always rejoice to hear of your being still employed in experimental researches into nature, and of the success you meet with. The rapid progress true science now makes, occasions my regretting sometimes that I was born so soon: it is impossible to imagine the height to which may be carried, in a thousand years, the power of man over matter; we may perhaps learn to deprive large masses of their gravity, and give them absolute levity for the sake of easy transport. Agriculture may diminish its labour and double its produce; all diseases may by sure means be prevented or cured (not excepting even that of old age), and our lives lengthened at pleasure even beyond the antediluvian standard. Oh! that moral science were in as fair a way of improvement; that men would cease to be wolves to one another; and that human beings would at length learn what they now improperly call humanity!" —Benjamin Franklin, letter to

Dr Priestley, February 8, 1780, found in *Memoirs of Benjamin Franklin* (1845)

Again, let me reiterate, I emphatically believe we are in a climate change. I know that climate change is a periodic occurrence on this planet. I know that CO^2 levels are at all-time highs (as recorded in 2008), and I know that this CO^2 elevation is detrimental to public health—especially those with respiratory disabilities. But I also know that it is a tropospheric phenomenon, an occurrence in a closed system where gases combine and dissolve, where oxygen is needed for human and animal life and carbon dioxide is needed for plant life; this a self-regulating system that has lasted for hundreds of millions of years. It is not going to fail now.

Climate change requires the involvement of the whole system: tropospheric, stratospheric, mesospheric, heliospheric, ionospheric, magnetospheric, protonospheric, and exospheric. Our problem is that we don't know enough about their roles because we are focused on the anthropocentric area and not on the whole cause. My hope is that we will return to science, not demagoguery, and find out what we need to know to survive this change.

The problems in the scientific community are a cause for concern; we have lost the idea of discovery, and we have moved into the *business* of science. Young graduate students no longer seek to follow their interests; they are directed to areas were the college or university can find grant money. They do their doctoral thesis on a subject that will make money for the institution but, in the end, be worth less than what they would have found if they had followed their heart. This can bottleneck growth and lead to fractious splits in the departments. This dilemma is not limited to American scientific endeavor by any means—it is worldwide.

In America, though, we are very focused on applications research rather than pure scientific research. The reason for that is a government, and even private organizations, want to be able to show some specific application for the money they give in grants. This is understandable, but limiting; real scientific breakthroughs are not going to come from applications research. Pure research, the leading edge of finding out how and why things work the way they do, is the path to real scientific knowledge and real understanding that leads to important and beneficial changes in our society. The problem of having politicians and bureaucrats decide who gets grants and what grants are given for is yet another of the deficiencies of our system of governance. The leading edge of scientific exploration is not in America anymore; it is at CERN, Switzerland. There scientists are looking for the "God particle," better known as the "Higgs boson." Professor Peter Higgs, a modest man, certainly would not call it the "God Particle," lest he offend someone, but the discovery and study of this one particle may tell us how the universe and everything in it is put together. He first formulated the theory behind the subatomic particle named after him in the 1960s, and for almost half a century it has remained as elusive as stardust. That could all change, however, when one of the world's biggest experiments is conducted deep beneath the Alpine meadows on the Franco-Swiss border, the home of the European Centre for Nuclear Research (CERN) near Geneva. Within a 27 km-long, circular tunnel, atom will be smashed into atom at something approaching the speed of light. The machine, called the Large Hadron Collider (LHC), is built to produce energy levels expected to be powerful enough to shake out the elusive Higgs boson from its seemingly inescapable prison within the atomic nucleus.

The Higgs boson is just one of the discoveries that the LHC is expected to make. The international team of physicists behind the project believes that the LHC will almost certainly produce a jewel box of discoveries that will light up the infinitesimally small world of subatomic physics. Another major objective of the LHC is to discover super-symmetry particles—symmetrical particles of the particles we already know. Super-symmetry refers to the "grand dance" of particles in the universe. We know of about a dozen subatomic particles, which have exotic names such as quark, lepton, and neutrino. Yet for every kind of particle, there may a super-symmetrical partner. The trouble is, we can only see one of the partners in each dancing couple, with the "significant others" remaining invisible. If super-symmetry is confirmed by the LHC, it will help scientists toward the ultimate goal of a unified theory for the fundamental forces of nature—in particular the force of gravity, which so far lies outside the realm of the forces known at the quantum level of subatomic particles. It is impossible to speculate what that could open up to us in terms of technology, but anti-gravity, interstellar space travel, even time travel are some of the things dreamed about. Promising research on the control of gravitons with weak magnetic fields is developing and could bring another age of exploration and development that would exceed our initial space race to the moon.

My point here is not to give you a science lesson, but to acquaint you with the reason why this research is being done at CERN and not in the United States. We do not lack the intellect to know that this research is important, and we did not lack the drive to try and be first, but we *do* lack a political system able to respond. Back in the 1980s the idea of building a Superconducting Super Collider (SSC) here in the United States, one bigger than the one at Fermi Labs in Illinois, was a scientific and political hot potato. There was great competition among the states acquire it. The competition was so intense that it actually slowed down the process of building, but finally it was awarded to Texas. Construction began on the SSC in the vicinity of Waxahachie, Texas. But after many years and many dollars, Congress decided not to continue the effort. We had sunk about $2 billion into the structure when it was halted in 1993; the anticipated price tag was $4.4 billion, which compares favorably to the CERN facility, which cost about $5 billion. Allegations of corruption and mismanagement abounded during the time of the construction, but it actually fell to a division in Congress on the budget bill, i.e. partisan politics. A singular lack of vision regarding what is really important characterizes all too many of the debates in Congress. Our two political parties seem to be incapable of getting anyone to run for elected office that has either vision or competence.

In addition to the party problems, for many years now there has been a spirit of xenophobia in the halls of science, especially in the academic circles. This has contributed to a significant loss of contribution to the expanding knowledge base. The xenophobia I'm referring to is not to foreign influence as it is to anything not invented here. It is understood that in any investigative pursuit there will arise disagreements as to what the data means, how to interpret it, and even whether it is valuable. That is to be expected, and for many years these disagreements were the kindling for ever greater advancements because honest and open discussion took place. In the past few decades this view of how science should work has changed. A degree of intolerance has been admitted, usually around some dogmatic attempt to prove that a given theory or belief is right. One of the more disturbing trends is to place that opinion that I have to be right in the way of openness and exchange, not unlike the political partisan debates that persist amiss the great depression of the 21st century.

"The science of government is my duty.... I must study politics and war that my sons may have liberty to study mathematics and philosophy. My sons ought to study mathematics and philosophy, geography, natural history, naval architecture, navigation, commerce, and agriculture, in order to give their children a right to study painting, poetry, music, architecture, statuary, tapestry, and porcelain." — John Adams, letter to Abigail Adams, (1780)

A much publicized theory called "string theory" was at the heart of one of these instances, and it caused a lot of disruption and unnecessary stagnation. The proponents of string theory strongly believed it was the way forward and made strenuous effort to promote it. They succeeded in gaining acceptance in academic circles, and as new adherents came forth over several decades, even became the dominate proponents in most academic institutions. They became department heads, acquired study grants, and began to exclude anyone who didn't agree with them. Eventually, graduate students in physics couldn't *not* promote string theory; they simply did not get graduate slots—and certainly not assistantships—that way. If you were a budding professor and didn't give the necessary lip service to the theory, you became ostracized by your peers; you weren't going to get tenure, and you would be lucky to even get a fair review of your teaching skills. The basic problem is that, while string theory does produce some elegant mathematical expressions and seems to be consistent within its own boundaries, it has yet to provide a provable theory of anything or to give us a hypothesis we could actually test anytime in the near future. So we had a tale full of sound and fury, signifying nothing.

This is why arguments over scientific data and what they mean must not be stopped by some politician (or scientist who wants money) saying the debate is over. The lack of progress that occurred in the field of physics during the time string theory dominated our academic institutions is appalling. The lost opportunity, even the lost careers, occasioned by this myopic obsession cannot be measured. In science, as in other fields, we simply cannot exclude the broader view in favor of the consensus view.

It is paradoxical that in a time when our education system is screaming for better scores in science and math and our government, our businesses, and our private scientific institutions are crying out for more engineers and scientists, we have a structure in the scientific community that is relentlessly closed to all but members of the fraternity. No matter what your discipline in science or engineering, you are subject to peer review of your work, be it by the American Society of Chemical Engineers, the American Institute of Electrical Engineers, the American Physical Society, The American Geophysical Union, the American Astronomical Society, etc. The problem arises when someone who does not belong to these societies tries to investigate their body of knowledge. Let's say a nine-year-old girl develops a keen interest in geophysics—perhaps inspired by her science teacher, her parents, or even a television show. She is, at nine, highly capable of searching the web and finds the American Geophysical Society website. She finds it both confusing and disorganized, but she persists and hits on a subject of interest. She selects it and opens it, but finds that to read the paper she has to pay $9.00. What she certainly won't find is a page for young kids to learn and to satisfy their curiosity. These organizations don't think they need to be responsible for that. Moreover it doesn't stop with the child seeking to find information. Let's say you are a chemist in a medical lab and you need to find information on the origin of certain chemicals; you go to that same site the child went to and find you are also denied access, despite the fact that your tax dollars fund most of their activities. The interdisciplinary exchange of information is hurt by this exclusivity and lays the foundations for its own collapse when no American children are interested in joining its ranks anymore

That sad prospect is the path we are taking in science, and it will not benefit anyone if we continue on it. Let's get politics out of science and get science back to discovery instead of lamenting the situation as described below:

"Yes," he said. "But [the solutions to problems in solid geometry such as the duplication of the cube] do not seem to have been discovered yet." "There are two reasons for this," I said. "Because no city holds these things in honour, they are investigated in a feeble way, since they are difficult; and the investigators need an overseer, since they will not find the solutions without one. First, it is hard to get such an overseer, and second, even if one did, as things are now those who investigate these things would not obey him, because of their arrogance. If however a whole city, which did hold these things in honour, were to oversee them communally, the investigators would be obedient, and when these problems were investigated continually and with eagerness, their solutions would become apparent."
—Plato, The Republic 528 B.C.

HOW DO WE FIX THIS?

Certainly greed, cliquishness, and one-tract minded obsession aren't a problem in science alone, but it is a problem that could dismantle science as we have been blessed to know it, if it is not stopped. Disagreeable as it might be, the scientific process is one that must have critical evaluation in order to validate its findings and to advance its knowledge. Without critical review science will fall apart, and there will be no process at all. The curse of this age, the paradigm of greed and power, is not just a destroyer of political and economic systems but of all systems. If science is to continue its long reign of respectability and objectivity it must remove itself from any political or economic motivation. To do this it will have to pursue funding from private rather than public sources. The public money comes with too many strings and is given with too high of expectations. Private funding often comes with strings and high expectations, but it is the lesser of two evils in this case.

The future of scientific investigation cannot be a future tied to politics. The apparatus of grant writing and funds-seeking lobbying has to be dismantled, and a new paradigm of pure research and civil evaluation must take its place. The stakes are high, as we have noted; it was the advances of science in the 1950–60s that made the growth in the job market of today possible. The American Middle Class has a large stake in the outcome of these advances, but pushing for government to carry the ball on this will in no way get a positive return on the money invested. The role of any new political reality will be to keep science and politics separated.

Chapter 9
Health Care

RETIREMENT AND PENSION FUNDS

An unusual feature of the American health care system is that it is provided to the worker by his employer. Among the countries that do have health insurance for their populations, the United States is one of the few who ties this to the employer. Let's take a look at some interesting comparisons.

Table 10: Health Systems Main Source of Financing

Most industrialized countries have established hybrid systems in which the public sector, which has the greater share of responsibility, works alongside the private sector, both in the funding of health care ...

	Health system's main source of financing		
	Taxes	Social Security Funds	Private Insurance
Australia (1992)	✓		
Canada (1990)	✓		
Denmark (1993)	✓		
France (1990)		✓	
Germany (1989)		✓	
Italy (1988)	✓		
Japan (1991)		✓	
Netherlands (1983)		✓	
Norway	✓		
Sweden	✓		
Switzerland (1991)			✓
United Kingdom (1994)	✓		
United States (1990)			✓

Source: Blanchette, Claude, "Public and Private Sector Involvement in Health Care Systems: An International Comparison," Bulletin 43/3E, Library of Parliament, 1997

2

Only two countries shown here tie the health care of their citizens to their citizens' employers: Switzerland and the United States. Most other countries fund health care through general taxes, although some include it in social security programs. It is obvious that if you are unemployed, you cannot afford a health insurance payment of $500–$1,200 per month (depending on how many dependents you have). It would be clear to an idiot that people will conserve their funds during that time to pay the mortgage or rent and to keep food on the table. That this would not be realized by our representatives in Washington is impossible. But the 20 percent pay the bill to get them elected, so if the insurers want it tied to the employers and the employers want it that way too, then the consitituents are the ones who get shortchanged. Actually, if you live in a country where the taxpayer picks up your health insurance, your pension, your life insurance, and so forth, then the idea that you wouldn't be able to pay the mortage and put food on the table might seem strange. The Elite may not understand this very well, but the 80 percent certainly do. This whole idea of having the employer pick up half or more of the employees health insurance is a clear illustration of the mind-set of our representatives in Washington. They don't see you as their constitutents – they see you as the surfs of the corporations who pay the contributions to their campaigns. The constitutents are an after thought.

Table 11: Main Delivey Entity of Hospital Health Care

... and in the delivery of hospital care

	Main Delivery Entity of Hospital Health Care (as percentage of hospital beds)		
	Public	Non-Profit	Private
Australia (1992)	75	---	25
Canada (1990)	98	---	2
Denmark (1993)	Most	---	---
France (1990)	65	16	19
Germany (1989)	51	35	14
Italy (1988)	80	20	0
Japan (1991)*	19	---	81
Netherlands (1983)	15	85	0
Norway	Most	---	---
Sweden	Most	---	---
Switzerland (1991)*	46	32	22
United Kingdom (1994)*	5	90	5
United States (1990)**	27	59	14

* As percentage of hospitals ** As percentage of acute-care hospital beds
Source: Blanchette, Claude, "Public and Private Sector Involvement in Health Care Systems: An International Comparison," Bulletin 438E, Library of Parliament, 1997   [3]

Tying our health care to an employer can be a serious problem when the employer lays you off. Most other countries seem to have realized that this method isn't a good way to fund health care. But in the United States, the private health insurance industry has a very large following in Congress, so anything that might disturb the industry's profit is forbidden. Logic be damned. Also, it is of great importance to the Political-Financial Complex that citizens do not have any incentive to live free, so making it almost impossibly expensive for them to buy private health insurance ensures the dependance of the working class on the corporate structure and makes them more easily held hostage by the medical needs of their families. Of course the same is true of disability insurance, life insurance, and pension plans. If your entire system of compensation is arranged to keep the working class in-line by making them dependent on large corporate employers, then you certainly wouldn't want to tie health insurance to the tax base or to Social Security. My God, that is socialism, with the citizens actually free from corporate control. How would we ever maintain our American values if our citizens were free?

The arguments for employer centered health care are not resonating very much with the fifty-one million people in the United States who have no health insurance. Whether you have to wait in line for medical care or whether you may not get that elective surgrey when you wanted it doesn't mean a thing to those who are uninsured. They know the arugment is about power and who is going to control them, not about the health of their sick baby.

Table 12: Percentage of Total Population with Public Insurance

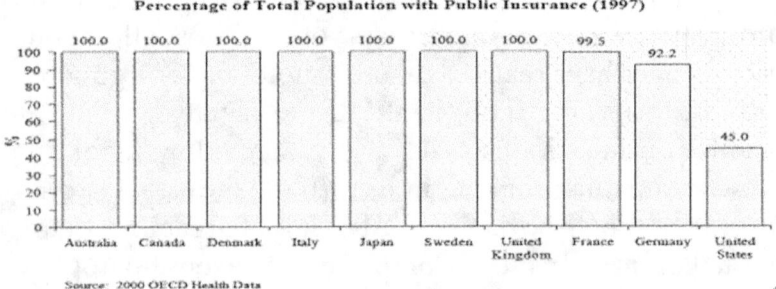

*With the exception of Germany and the United States, most of the industrialized countries have **universal** publicly funded health care systems*

Percentage of Total Population with Public Insurance (1997)

Source: 2000 OECD Health Data

4

Opponents of universal health care programs are quick to cite numerous problems with socialized medicine in other countries. They are against such a plan, they say, because other countries have multiple flaws in their programs, including limited access to expensive tests like MRIs, long waiting periods for surgeries, and delay of care until medical conditions are too far advanced for treatment.

Immigrants who have participated in such health care, however, often tell a different story, especially after they experience the high cost of medical care in America. A

German immigrant recently spoke about this very issue. He acknowledged that they paid much higher taxes in Germany, but insisted that they had no problem getting whatever health care was needed. The French have made similar claims, admitting that they get a lower salary because employers of a certain size are required to contribute to the national health care system, but they claim that the health care they need is readily available.

The debate rages on, but the real argument is not whether we need "better" health care in America. What we need is more accessible health care at a more reasonable cost. The two issues are not even remotely similar. In contrast to most of Europe, American health care is nothing more than a practice in treating the symptoms of diseases. There is little attempt to actually cure anything, and there is even less emphasis on prevention of disease in the first place.

Instead of focusing only on the pros and cons of a national health care system, we need to completely revise our attitudes and practices toward good health in general. Simply funding a massive nationwide program that will keep paying the out-of-control prices on prescription drugs and the inflated charges to hospitals and clinics will do nothing more than finalize the road to bankruptcy down which America seems to be headed.

To demonstrate the need for change, consider the following:

America has one of the highest rates of chronic diseases, second only to Australia.

The most rapidly growing disease among children in America is cancer.

Obesity and diabetes are at epidemic levels among the nation's young people.

The healthiest—and smallest—segment of America is the senior population, particularly those who take no prescription drugs.

The recommended levels of cholesterol were arrived at by the drug companies, not by physicians or any real medical results of patients.

For the first time in history, American young people are dying before their much older parents and grandparents.

The number of chronic ailments among American patients could be radically reduced by a change in diet or exercise or by the removal of toxins from our homes, environments, or food products.

In short, other countries have health care models that could work in America, but unless the overall approach to health and wellness undergoes a radical change—beginning with the medical schools—any attempt to imitate a European system will do little more than bankrupt the country. Removing junk food from our schools, taking pesticides from our food, getting hormones and antibiotics out of our meat products, removing the crowding and unsanitary conditions that large corporate food processors prefer would go a long way to making America healthier. But so long as your congressmen take bribes (contributions) from the giant corporate food conglomerates nothing in this picture is going to change.

The private health insurance market is a mess. It is supposed to cover the sick but instead competes to insure the healthy. It employs platoons of adjusters whose sole job is to get out of paying for needed services that members thought were covered. In fact, multimillion dollar bonuses are awarded annually to top health care executives as incentive to deny coverage to policy holders who thought they are covered. Over one third of families living below the poverty line are uninsured. More than nine million children in America lack health insurance. Eighteen thousand people die each year because they are uninsured. The current system is increasingly inaccessible to many poor and lower-middle-class people, and those lucky enough to have coverage are paying steadily more and/or receiving steadily fewer benefits.

Yet your taxpayer dollars go to cover an enormous number of research and development projects aimed at curing the nation's aliments. Problem is, they never do. It is a recognized fact that the biggest health problem facing Americans is obesity. One major health problem resulting from obesity is diabetes. Do you know that government funding—not private sector funding, just government funding—for diabetes research has exceeded $400,000,000 every year for the past two decades? Yet we have not seen any significant advance in treatment for either juvenile or old-age onset diabetes since 1922 when two Canadian scientists discovered insulin. Think of the outcry if NASA funded a project for two decades for that same amount of money and wound up with nothing to show for it. You can be very sure their funding would be cut—and cut sharply—but that just doesn't happen in the world of "medical research." You can't demand results and you can't cut budgets because the medical research community have a whole legion of supporters. They have strung people along by making promises that are never fulfilled, and they write their congressmen every time the question of reduced funding comes up. This naturally leads to conspiracy theories that claim we have had a cure for diabetes since the 1980s, but because it is so lucrative for the pharmaceutical companies and the health care apparatus companies to treat diabetics, we do not allow that cure to be known. Normally I'm not a fan of conspiracy theories, but I think this one has some merit.

Recently, Congress spent months and months debating the revisions to the health care system proposed by President Obama. This debate had one defining characteristic—it was completely insincere. It was all for show. Congress knows we have the worse health care delivery system in the entire industrialized world; debating that is foolhardy. I call the debate insincere because more than half of the members of Congress had signed pledges with the health insurance and pharmaceutical industries indicating they would not vote for any health care reform bill. So no real reform could be voted on. What passed as a so-called national health care reform bill was nothing more than a continuation of the same old thing, with less than 1 percent of our population being added to the plan. It was a complete farce. Read this from Health Care for America Now:

Today, the health insurance industry got what it paid for in the 2010 elections, a Republican majority determined to let the insurance companies off the hook and kill the new law's strong consumer protections, such as the ban on denying sick people care. This law is already making a real difference in the lives of millions of Americans by stopping health insurers from denying care, dropping people when they're sick and jacking up rates anytime they please. The Republicans have scheduled a fast-track repeal vote next week to satisfy their extremist Tea Party base and to pay back the health insurance companies that funded their election campaigns.

"At the same time Speaker Boehner railed sanctimoniously against 'fast legislating' and called for 'allowing additional amendments and open debate,' he was preparing to skip the usual legislative processes and rush the repeal vote. Boehner said he and his party were "humbled" by the American people, but it's hubris that's driving the Republicans' reckless effort to rush a vote to give our health care back to the insurance companies.

"What do the Republicans want to replace the new law with? Nothing. They're referring that question to House committees that will deliberate for months and play political football with our lives and health.

"Repeal means letting the insurance companies run roughshod over consumers, deny our care and raise our rates with impunity. When the Republicans vote for repeal on Jan. 12, they'll be telling seniors to pay back the $250 donut hole checks they received to help buy prescription drugs. They'll be booting young adults off their parents' health plans. And they'll be taking away the American people's newly won freedom from the fear of bankruptcy caused by crushing medical bills. We're finally getting the insurance companies off our backs and the first thing the Republicans want to do is let them off the hook."

Notice though that the one provision that did make it through was the requirement that every citizen must buy health insurance. Since the option for the government to create universal health care coverage was removed from the final version of the bill, who do you think actually benefited from all that hot air they blow in Washington? You're right; it was the private insurance industry, a senior member of the Political-Industrial Complex. It is interesting to hear Senator Boehner complain that President Obama is inciting "class warfare". I got news for you Senator Boehner the 20% you represent has been conducting class warfare on the American Middle Class for over 100 years.

"I consider the foundation of the Constitution as laid on this ground that 'all powers not delegated to the United States, by the Constitution, nor prohibited by it to the states, are reserved to the states or to the people.' To take a single step beyond the boundaries thus specially drawn

around the powers of Congress is to take possession of a boundless field of power, no longer susceptible of any definition." Thomas Jefferson, Opinion on the Constitutionality of a National Bank, February 15, 1791

Table 13: Health Indicators

Canada and the United States rank poorly on some health status indicators, although Canada outperforms the United States

Rank	Health Indicators		
	Infant Mortality Rate per 1,000 births (1997*)	Cancer Mortality Rate per 100,000 persons (1995**)	Heart Disease mortality [1] per 100,000 persons (1995***)
1	Japan (3.7)	Japan (156)	France (173)
2	Sweden (4.0)	Sweden (158)	Japan (178)
3	Germany (4.8)	Australia (177)	Canada (227)
4	France (4.8)	United States (183)	Australia (255)
5	Australia (5.3)	Canada (184)	Italy (271)
6	Denmark (5.6)	Germany (184)	Sweden (273)
7	United Kingdom (5.9)	France (186)	United States (280)
8	Canada (6.0)	Italy (195)	United Kingdom (282)
9	Italy (6.2)	United Kingdom (192)	Germany (308)
10	United States (7.8)	Denmark (227)	Denmark (328)

* 1995 for Italy, 1996 for Canada, Denmark, United States and Sweden
** 1993 for Denmark and Italy, 1996 for United States and Sweden, 1997 for Germany and United Kingdom
*** 1993 for Denmark and Italy, 1994 for Japan, 1996 for United States and Sweden and 1997 for Germany and United Kingdom
1 Includes ischaemic heart diseases, acute myocardial infarction, cerebrovascular diseases and others.   17
Source: 2000 OECD Health Data

When it comes to health care plans, the country that the United States is most often compared to is Canada. The insurance companies and their lackeys (media and congressmen) want you to believe that health care in Canada don't measure up. Take a look at the above comparison of the three most important measures of a health care system and ask yourself two questions: (1) Why would they say Canada's system doesn't measure up when Canada is ahead of us in two out of three categories? (2) Why aren't we comparing ourselves to Japan, France, or Sweden? Because the insurance companies and the Wall Street brokers own our government, discussion on any important matter is going to be limited to what they want to talk about, not to what is actually pertinent. They frame the discussion to speak to anything except what is really important. As long as we do not have a free press, we will not have a real discussion about health care in this country.

One thing about Canada that you will never hear is that they have no national debt. That's right: no debt at all, nada, none. Yet they are a full member of NATO, their soldiers are standing beside ours in almost every war we fight (Iraq being a notable exception—but who could blame them, except maybe all the self-styled 20 percenters who call themselves patriots). No doubt they have higher taxes—but the taxes don't go to pay for the idiots on Wall Street, and they don't go to make sure the rich get richer and the poor get nothing. They actually spread the wealth around. If we weren't so arrogant, we might learn something from our neighbors to the north. It does appear that we have taken a page from our neighbors to the south though. Our southern neighbors in North America certainly do have national debt, and they like to call themselves a democracy—but just 10 percent of the population has 38% of the country's wealth – sound familiar? They have instituted corruption to such an extent that you have to bribe the mailman to get your mail. Their political parties are so power hungry that they have engaged in civil war almost every time they have had an election. We're not far behind them really.

We have in this country a Social Security system that was started in 1934 by Franklin D. Roosevelt. Of course, it was a response to the Great Depression of the twentieth century, and at the time Social Security had a promising future. The problem is Congress, having started such a major financial sop, just couldn't keep their hands off of it. They always had a war or a financial crisis created by Wall Street that gave them an excuse to dip into the Social Security fund in order to keep the nation solvent. So instead of being a steadily building fund as any other pension fund would have been, it has been a fund barely able to survive into the twenty-first century, and one that is likely to default unless the government raises the contribution levels again. Doesn't it just seem like everything the two parties get their greedy little hands on turns to... Well, you know what it turns to, don't you?

In the next year or so, Congress will "revamp" the Social Security system yet again. It will raise the amount withheld from your paycheck, and it will raise the age at which you can retire. The Republicans will say it was necessary to keep the fund afloat, and the Democrats will say that the involuntary tax increase that this represents is part of how they are ensuring the future solvency of the system for the average American. The media will get into lengthy discussions with pundits from both parties debating whether or not Social Security has really been saved from default. Not one of them will point out that Social Security wouldn't have to be saved if Congress had kept their greedy hands off of it, like it was originally set up to work. Most certainly no one will point out that the hundreds and hundreds of billions pilfered from the fund by politicians from both parties went directly to aid their elite buddies on Wall Street. What we're saying here is get ready for another onslaught of hot air filled with half-truths, unspoken real truths, and out-and-out lies. So what else is new?

Taking their cue from Congress, states, counties, and local governments have also set up various pension funds—excluding their own employees from the mandatory Social Security tax—and like the federal government, they have continuously underfunded it to the point of default. So now the taxpayer gets a double whammy from all levels of government. Not only does this poor soul have to bail out the Social Security fund that the federal government has pilfered, but to cover the largest of our state and local governments, the taxpayer will also be allowed to bail out the state pension funds that are going to people who never paid a dime into the Social Security fund. It is interesting to note here that the majority of state governments put balanced budget requirements into their constitutions, yet failed to recognize that although the budgets could be balanced every year as long as the economy was growing they would fall like a house of cards once the economy retracted. I don't think you can legislate good management practices or the idea that a fiduciary responsibility is inherent in public service, but it would be worth a try.

Unfortunately, I really don't have to point out the next level of incompetence to millions of Americans who have lost their pension benefits—but I should at least mention it. By now we see that it is a game of "monkey see, monkey do," so of course the big corporations have followed right along in the pattern: the World Coms and the Enrons run by the Elite have squandered taxpayers' pensions on every scheme ever invented by a conman, just to be sure that they spend ever last dime before they slip off to their private island retreats or hide out in one of their ten ostentatious homes—strategically placed all over the world.

As everyone knows, for the Elite 20 percent, using money that does not belong to you to cover expenses for items that have no intrinsic value does not get you indicted like it would if you were a member of the 80 percent; that is, of course, how Congress intended it. I hope by now no one reading this would object if I made a sweeping statement about all of this; whenever you elect persons who believe they are allowed by right of being elected to make decisions that favor those they want to favor, you will see corruption flourish. Our two-party political system simply does not work for 80 percent of our population, and it is doubtful that any system of representation will ever work for the majority of the population.

One last thing... I should mention this because it will give you an understanding of just how accurate it is to call these people elitist and to say they view the rest of us as their serfs. Congress has exempted every one of its members from paying into Social Security; they do not pay for Medicare, they have a much better system: it is entirely funded by the taxpayers and it provides them complete vesture in a retirement plan after just one term in office, but they did not exempt themselves from the Affordable Health Care for America Act (HR 3962) of 2009. "The only health plans that the Federal Government may make available to Members of Congress and congressional staff with respect to their service as a Member of Congress or congressional staff shall be health plans that are — (I) created under this Act (or an amendment made by this Act); or (II) offered through an Exchange established under this Act (or an amendment made by this Act), from PolitiFacts. com". And you thought we were just disgruntled, negative old goats!

HOW DO WE FIX THIS?

Sorry to say, but we must have an amendment to the Constitution that will prohibit Congress from passing legislation from which they are exempt. If they do, they will be immediately recalled. Then we need an amendment that will prohibit Congress from passing mandatory participation legislation of any type and repealing any such laws they have already passed. We then need an amendment that requires federal, state, and local governments to fund their pension plans from the pockets of their employees— including Congress—and that makes it a criminal offense to remove any retirement money from the fund. The penalty for doing so is life in prison. To ensure compliance, we need to set up a commission with judicial powers—a commission elected directly by the people, not appointed by a politician—to regulate the retirement and pension fund industry and to ensure that all of the funds are properly invested in real securities that are from American companies only. We need these funds to grow our own industrial base, not that of some other country.

So how do we fund a national retirement fund and a national health care system? We fund it like other sensible nations have funded it: we create a sales tax to cover it. No more private insurance companies siphoning us off into groups and refusing to cover some groups and maximizing profits on other groups. No more uninsured citizens, and no more refusals to pay for legitimate medical procedures. And the most important thing we have to do is get proactive about preventive medicine and start training doctors in private practice how to monitor and advise us on healthy lifestyle choices. But we will not make them mandatory. You know I believe if we had not had such a corrupt system created by the Political-Financial Complex we would have seen an insurance industry that was actually competitive, brought forth real insurance products that would have made it possible for every American to be insured. But because they could buy congress and they could write their own legislation to limit competition and inflate profits they did not have to be competitive and they lost their pluck for capitalism.

Let's finally get this right. We are the inheritors of a system of governance that was set up with checks and balances to ensure our *freedom*. It is not designed to keep us safe. If it was, we would never have ventured westward and opened up this continent to settlement—it would have been too dangerous. We are the home of the free and the land of the brave, not the home of the safe and the land of the woozy. That clearly means that for all of us who actually think clearly, we do not mandate anything to a citizen that he or she does not get to vote on. And if we follow the blueprint in this book, we will get to that point again.

What the past forty years have taught us is that it doesn't matter how carefully and how expertly you set up your checks and balances. The system you devise will not work if the people who run it are addicted to greed and power and believe that they know better than everyone else how to live life—so they are going to make everyone live it their way, Constitution be dammed. They will ignore the Constitution, pass laws to favor themselves and their friends, and bombard the populace with lies, half-truths, and red herrings to be sure no one catches on. But having said all that, we do also have to say, it helps the greedy and powerful pull this off if the population in question is a herd of donkeys.

Chapter 10
Religion

66**B**elieving with you that religion is a matter which lies solely between man and his God, that he owes account to none other for his faith or his worship, that the legislative powers of government reach actions only, and not opinions, I contemplate with sovereign reverence that act of the whole American people which declared that their legislature should 'make no law respecting an establishment of religion, or prohibiting the free exercise thereof, 'thus building a wall of separation between church and State."
—Thomas Jefferson, letter to a Committee of the Danbury Baptist Association, Connecticut, January 1, 1802

The principle stated above has been an integral part of our system of governance from the very beginning. I could quote John Adams, George Washington, and Ben Franklin on this issue, and all quotes would agree that a founding principle of our revolution was the separation of church and state. They had very determined ideas about this, and all the attempts by Christian ministers since to say America was founded as a Christian nation is just wrong. Many of our Founders were Masons and quite proud to say it. The Masons have been mystified in the media in modern times and made to look like some kind of cult. Nothing could be further from the truth. They are a secret community service organization, nonracial, that looks at the community standing of an individual before he can be sponsored for membership. They are not publicity seekers, but they accomplish a lot of good in every community they serve. They are made up of many diverse denominations. They are focused on truths that are timeless and common to all the great religions. The beliefs of Freemasonry can be boiled down to these three simple concepts. Masons are taught to believe in:

- **Brotherly love:** Love for each other and for all mankind

- **Relief:** Charity for others and mutual aid for fellow Masons

- **Truth:** The search for answers to the universal questions of morality and the salvation of the soul that only a man's individual faith and his relationship with God can provide

Their members exhibit a discipline that is admirable; rarely has anyone who is a Mason been involved in any public scandal. That is why the press, ever circling like sharks looking for blood in the water, has chosen to mystify them, because they can't degrade them. The principles that many Founders held were Masonic and this naturally reflected itself in our Declaration of Independence and in our Constitution. They definitely were not Fundamentalist Christian ideals.

It is interesting to observe that if Jesus Christ came back today and began preaching his message of peace and love, the first people to attack him and try to crucify him either physically or verbally would be the Southern right wing, so called, Fundamentalist Christians. Why do I say that, let's take a look at why. The American Christian fundamentalist movement began as a reaction to mainline Protestant churches teaching modernist challenges, including biblical criticism and interpretation. In response, between 1910 and 1915 conservative scholars from Princeton Theological Seminary published a series of twelve books titled *The Fundamentals,* which reaffirmed biblical inerrancy and attacked biblical criticism. Christian fundamentalists teach the literal interpretation of scripture and hold to key Christian doctrines, including Jesus' birth, death, and resurrection, and salvation from our sins through the grace of God by having faith in Jesus Christ. Besides these doctrines, Christian Fundamentalism is also marked by its conservative social stances, including the refusal to smoke, drink alcohol, or dance. In recent decades, Christian Fundamentalism has also been characterized by its criticism of liberal social and political policies most notably legalized abortion, evolution taught in schools, and gay and lesbian rights. The two guiding principles of Christian fundamentalism are therefore inerrancy of the Bible and the unallowable thought of critical analysis of the text, i.e. all things must be accepted on faith. We have no conflict with this, it is their right as Americans to express their faith in any way they want to express it. The problem comes in when they combine their faith with a determination to force it upon everyone else. This is especially true in a secular society where we do not allow state religions. So if you believe abortion is wrong, then you have every right to believe that; but if others do not believe that then they have every right to believe what they believe without you trying to make what they believe a criminal offense.

Remember one of the guiding forces of the American Constitution is the separation of church and state. When you promote your beliefs as law you are disrespecting the foundations of the nation that gave you the right to express your religious beliefs without interference. We would say that this is a very dangerous position to take. Christian Fundamentalism is not the only religious belief that its adherents want to make into law and force upon their fellow citizens. Once you cross that bridge it automatically burns behind you and you will find yourself in a world that you will not like. What if, and only as an intellectual exercise, we had an Islamic religious movement in America that swept through the country and they gained majority voting status? Would you like to live under Sharia Law? Or what if Catholicism took over; would you want to live under Canon law? Maybe the Mormons catch fire with the public and they make their laws supreme. The promise of America is that religion will not influence politics, not the other way around. Anyone who would overturn this principle will live to regret it. The Founding Fathers were not the only ones who believed in this principle, "And Jesus answering said to them, Render to Caesar the things that are Caesar's, and to God the things that are God's. And they marveled at him" Mark 12:17. But let's not take it out of context let's read the whole exchange as given in the Bible. "And they sent some of the Pharisees and Herodians to Him (read that as lawyers and politicians) in order to trap Him in a statement. And they came and said to Him, Teacher, we know that You are faithful, and defer to no one; for You are not partial to any, but teach the way of God in truth. Is it lawful to pay a poll-tax to Caesar, or not? Shall we pay or shall we not pay? But He knowing their hypocrisy, said to them, "Why are you testing Me? Bring Me a denarius to look at. And they brought one. And He said to them, Whose likeness and inscription is this? And they said to Him, Caesar's. And Jesus said to them 'Render to Caesar the things that are Caesar's, and to God the things that are God's' Mark 12 13-17." Does this not say that Jesus would have agreed with the Founding Fathers on separation of church and state? This is precisely the argument for really strengthening your faith by doing critical analysis. Without some form of critical analysis you are open to every type of flawed interpretation; when that happens you will find yourself arguing with Jesus on His own words.

It is likewise interesting that if Abraham Lincoln came back today, the Republican party would be the first to ostracize him for being too liberal, with Rush, "the attack dog" Limbaugh leading the way and his dutiful robot ditto heads nodding their heads in unison. So why do we say that?

"I see in the near future a crisis approaching that unnerves me and causes me to tremble for the safety of my country... corporations have been enthroned and an era of corruption in high places will follow."- Abraham Lincoln

Need I say more?

The marriage of these two, the Christian Fundamentalist and the conservative Republican, has produced a voting block of persons that are neither Christian nor Conservative. They dishonor both brands. It has also produced a body of law that is completely out of character with our Constitution and an anathema to a secular state. Even if you agree that children are a wonderful and joyous gift of God, as I do, you do not put that into your legal system. You don't do that because it is *your* belief; your belief is not everyone's belief, so it is not a proper expression of law in a secular state. Laws are the expression of commonly held beliefs; stealing is wrong, bribery is wrong, murder is wrong, kickbacks are wrong, rape is wrong, exploitation is wrong, judging others before you have the facts is wrong. We have these things in law because most of us agree they are wrong. But we do not all agree that abortion is wrong and all of the gatherings outside of Planned Parenthood clinics have not changed the public mind. The scientific fact is that we do not know when the soul enters the body, and your opinion is no better than anyone else's. The Bible clearly states that "breath" is the giver of life, as when God "breathed" life into Adam. My personal interpretation of that is that when the child takes its first breath he/she is alive, not before. But what does it matter what I believe? The point is I do not try to make my beliefs law. Why? Because that is against the Constitution. We have definitely separated church from state—read the First amendment, the cornerstone of our freedoms. If you can't support that, then you don't belong in the United States.

The last haven for Southern Jim Crowism is the Republican Party, and the last haven for pagan hatred, intolerance, aggression, and racism is the modern Southern Christian Fundamentalist political movement.

The Bible tells us that the only recorded time that the "Prince of Peace" lost it and became uncontrollably angry was when he was confronted with the "money changers" in the temple. "Money changers" are bankers. So Christians should have concluded that what makes God angry are greedy, deceitful, and selfish bankers. Apparently he can withhold his anger from almost anything else. That doesn't say much for bankers or their cohorts in crime, politicians.

The mix of religion, politics, and greed is the very cause of every war, every injustice, and every oppression the human race has seen in its roughly four thousand years of recorded history. This is not confined to the United States either. This combination rules almost every country on Earth.

It is interesting to observe that if the prophet Mohammed came back today and met with those who say they are his followers, he too would be appalled. And Osama bin Laden's followers would be the first to attack him; he wouldn't be conservative enough for them, he actually wants justice and freedom for his followers, not oppression and death if they miss even one the great Mullah's sanctions. Can you imagine his reaction to Sharia law? Holding slaves, raping the women of the men we don't like, raping women who happen to be without a male companion, mainly raping women whenever we feel like it, killing daughters if they don't do exactly what they are told and we calling it an "honor" killing? Oh, and teaching the children to hate all infidels, but especially the "People of the Book" and to kill them by any means possible. There should be no compunctions about killing believers or infidels. Wouldn't Mohammed be proud? If you think we are being unfair in these rape charges we suggest you contact Lara Logan, the CBS 60 Minutes reporter, who was covering the Egyptian Arab spring uprising and was grabbed by the crowd of men in Cairo's Tahrir Square and repeatedly raped until she was nearly killed. This incident shed a very bad light on Muslin men and on Sharia Law. It disgraced all Egyptians and their cause.

The Koran says all Muslims are one big happy family, following the same rules and doing exactly the will of Allah, yet the Wahhabi want to call all other beliefs but theirs heresy, and the Sunni hate the Shiites, and the Baath Party is a totalitarian nightmare wherever and whenever it appears. And almost all of our governments are run by strong men or "kings" who take everything for themselves and keep the people in poverty. Aren't you proud, Mohammed? The sheiks, caliphs, and mullahs can find a verse in the Koran to justify every one of these actions—that is what makes Islam so strong.

But, of course, it wouldn't be fair to leave it here with just Christians and Muslims: what about the Jews? I wonder what their father, Abraham, would think of the modern Jews. Do you think he would be pleased to know that they once prospered in the "land of milk and honey" but let jealousy destroy their peaceful existence when Joseph's brothers sold him into slavery in Egypt? That they all moved out of that land and came to be slaves themselves in Egypt? That Moses led them out of Egypt and back to Palestine, where they again prospered until jealousy reared its ugly head again? That they split up their kingdom after Solomon died into two parts that frequently warred on each other. Then they were all hauled off to Babylon to be slaves again but managed to come back and reestablish the kingdom, only to be subverted by the Romans, whom they invited in under the Maccabeus to help fight their enemies. This last time lead to the Diaspora after the Romans grew tired of their quarrelsome ways.

Now they are back in Palestine, this time because they bought the right from the French and British after the First World War and got lots of additional citizens after the Nazis and the Second World War. Oh, Father Abraham, aren't you proud of us? We made it back again and we learned a lot from our Nazi teachers. We now have a state that is for Jews only, just like the Third Reich was for Aryans only. We call our state a democracy, but you don't vote if you aren't a Israeli. You don't have any property rights if you aren't a Israeli. We will take your property whenever we want it, and you can only be a second-class citizen if you aren't a Israeli, so what we really have is a modern theocracy based on race and religion. We keep the native Palestinians in a constant state of war, refuse to negotiate with them, and thereby keep them as people without a country. We like it that way. Our good friends the Americans keep us supplied with all the latest weapons so we can subvert and suppress the Palestinians and keep all our Arab neighbors living in fear of us. Oh, Father Abraham, aren't you proud of us; we don't rely on our faith in God at all—we rely on our armaments. We don't try to negotiate with the Arabs—we just kill them. Oh yes, and we didn't learn anything from all those diasporas; we still are not united internally, and we still look to a powerful ally to keep our position in Palestine. You were God's friend and trusted in him for everything even unto killing you're firstborn, but we don't trust anybody.

There is another player in this religious charade that pretends to meet the spiritual needs of the masses; it is the Catholic Church. Now there is a piece of work. The people who brought us the heretic burnings, the Inquisition, the Crusades, the Holy Roman Empire, and a priesthood of organized, systemic pedophiles who used the church to both spread and cover up their lecherous ways. You should know that this is not a present-day phenomenon, but has been going on in the Catholic Church for over a thousand years. Did I mention they also claim to be infallible in matters of faith and morals, really infallible?

I suppose if you take young boys at the tender age of nine or ten and send them to a monastery to become priests, you might consider that you're playing with fire. Everyone who has ever raised a book on ancient Greek history knows that this system of taking young boys and having them raised by men is the surest path to homosexual behavior ever invented. So, surprise, surprise, the boys get abused and wind up doing the same to the next generation. Pedophilia was a way of life in Sparta; it produced a very well organized armed force that fought well together against overwhelming odds, but Sparta adopted this as a cultural norm. The parents of the boys given to the seminaries of the Catholic Church do not adopt this behavior as a cultural norm; in fact the societies they come from do not adopt it either. So it is illegal. Any parent, who knowingly puts a child in this structure should be arrested along with the church hierarchy that is covering it up. It is way past time that we started acting on this. Money does not substitute for innocence. It would be a real revelation to see were this puts the church when it comes time to separate the sheep from the goats.

Now we take these deeply flawed organizations purporting to be spiritual advisors to the world, mix them with politics, and get a formula for disaster. If your politics is your religion or vice versa, you have no politics and you certainly have no religion. Yet all over this country, the first to separate religion and politics, we have preachers, priests, rabbis, and imam telling their flocks who to vote for and who to deride. We even had a candidate for the Republican Party nomination for president, Pat Robinson, openly run on the platform of turning America into a Christian theocracy. As if that weren't what we created this country to prevent. To be sure politics is not improved by this, but the big loser is religion.

If we were able to bring Abraham, Jesus, and Mohammad back and ask them each why they began ministering to the people, it cannot be argued by any faithful follower of these men that they started doing what they did to create reform. These men were reformers. They were not political opportunists—they were not greedy, power hungry, self-absorbed, or hedonistic; they were humanitarian, compassionate reformers. They didn't tell their followers to strap bombs on and blow themselves up in a public market place, they didn't preach torturing and burning at the stake anyone who disagreed with them, and they didn't instruct their followers to disenfranchise both politically and economically anyone who was not of their faith. They saw the suffering the religious and political systems of their times were inflicting on the masses of the people, and they acted compassionately to stop it. They all risked their lives to save their people from oppression. That is the mark of leadership, which is the depth of spirituality, which is the divine spark in all of us.

Even though some like to think of Thomas Jefferson as not being a religious man he would beg to differ. **"And can the liberties of a nation be thought secure when we have removed their only firm basis, a conviction in the minds of the people that these liberties are the gift of God? That they are not to be violated but with his wrath? Indeed I tremble for my country when I reflect that God is just: that His justice cannot sleep forever."** —Thomas Jefferson, Notes on the State of Virginia, Query 18, 1781

Sometimes Ben Franklin is portrayed as an atheistic scientist and a man who was amoral, especially where women were concerned, but he too would like to set the record straight. **"It is that particular wise and good God, who is the Author and Owner of our system that I propose for the Object of my praise and adoration. For I conceive that He has in Himself some of those passions He has planted in us, and that, since He has given us reason whereby we are capable of observing His wisdom in the Creation, He is not above caring for us, being pleas'd with our praise and offended when we slight Him, or neglect His Glory. I conceive for many reasons that He is a good Being, and as I should be happy to have so wise, good and powerful a Being my Friend, let me consider in what Manner I shall make myself most acceptable to Him."** —Benjamin Franklin, Articles of Belief and Acts of Religion, November 20, 1728

It is an important point of comparison to contrast the thoughts of Jefferson and Franklin, Founders of our republic, on the attributes of God with the thoughts of modern religionists (Fundamentalist Christians, Wahhabi Muslims, and Zionist ideologists). The differences are more than substantial; they are deep, far-reaching, and philosophically incompatible. That same incompatible faith also exists between the Founders of these monotheistic religions and what the current professors of those same religions teach. The former is based on the belief that God is both just and good, the latter is based on the belief that God is vengeful, tyrannical, and filled with malice. Therein lies the cause of our present world dilemma. There has been significant growth in the human soul in the 235 years since the Declaration of Independence, but that growth was neither ubiquitous nor egalitarian. So we are struggling with people living in the twenty-first century who have a mental capacity rooted in a belief system that would make any medieval potentate blush with embarrassment if it was proclaimed in his name. It is precisely the root of all evil—even more than the love of money.

I think the most amazing thing is that people still subscribe to these religions and the subsequent belief systems they spawn. Such people make the word "masochist" seem weak. Suppose you are suffering with the loss of a loved one, a mentally disabled child, a long bout with a crippling and deadly disease, the brutal rape and murder of your lovely daughter; you go to your minister, priest, rabbi, or Inman and ask him or her for help in understanding this experience. What do you get? "None of us knows what the will of God is," "God is testing you," "It is the will of Allah," "We are meant to suffer," or "You have offended God; repent of your sins. What kind of dribble is that? It lacks any substance or any higher understanding. Abraham, Jesus, and Mohammad wouldn't ever have given you such an answer; their understanding was far higher than that. If you subscribe to this as your answer, you are not only missing the very teaching you say you believe in, you do not understand the nature of God as our forefathers clearly understood it. You do not belong in a modern democracy; you belong in a prison nation run by a totalitarian sadist. This, of course, is exactly what did happen and is happening to many of those with this belief. That is not coincidence.

Let us say you have endured one or more of the above mentioned tragedies in your life, you wake up one day, and you realize you have a deep resentment in your heart about these experiences. You seek spiritual council from a true councilor—what would you hear? It would go something like this: It is not wise to label everything that you experience good or bad. Life and the world are not really right or wrong, good or bad, true or false; it is much more connected than that. You should strive to see that connectedness and it will free you, even if it doesn't heal you.

You have the experience of resentment; it is an experience that can be overcome, but it is overcome more easily on a personal level than on a wider level, on the level where it hurts those you love, and on the level where it hurts humanity. If your spouse cheats on you, you may find forgiveness or not; if your child gets cancer, is treated with chemotherapy (tortured), and then dies anyway, that is much harder to forgive. It is hard to forgive because you are not trying to forgive an individual—you are trying to forgive God; you know the child did nothing to deserve that pain and suffering, and you know God did nothing to stop it. That is hard to forgive. Suppose you wake one morning and you hear on the news that there was a tornado in the next town up the road; the tornado hit at night, no one knew it was coming, many people in the next town died as a result, and one of the families that perished was your brother's family—all of them gone—with no rhyme or reason to it. That can build resentment, and it is not toward people; it is toward a God who would allow such things to happen. What kind of creation is this anyway? Even if you didn't know anyone at the scene of the disaster, such as the Indonesian, Haitian, or Japanese earthquakes, you still feel that deep resentment of the conditions of life on this planet and the total disregard of the Creator for his created.

The connecting link then is in the understanding you have of what this world and this life are designed to do. First, they are not designed to make everyone in every place follow some distorted and perverse ideology in lockstep. They are designed to allow you to experience who you are. So you are here experiencing resentment: you resent the misery that God has inflicted on you, your loved ones, and humanity in general. The resentment is so deep you just want to shout it out at God.

Your councilor suggests you see the whole picture; your resentment is a sure sign you are not some self-centered dote of an individual who cares for nothing but him or herself. You are compassionate, and you care for others—you couldn't feel that resentment if you didn't. You know who you are. In this experience of resentment you have defined yourself; that might be why you are here. Without the cause of your resentment you could not know this about yourself; you would remain undefined. If sixty or seventy years of life on this insane planet got you that knowledge, it was surely worth it. You came here undefined, without experience, and you were searching for who you are; you got one answer. The answer is unequivocal; the experience is valid. The emotion of resentment was real, and you have defined a part of yourself that will remain with you. The price was suffering, but we all knew it would be—we had to have the experience. The price made the experience; without the price the experience doesn't happen, you don't define yourself, and you don't know who you are. Now you can experience gratitude; you have made tremendous progress in your growth as a human being, and you have your loved ones to thank for bringing you the experience as well as God to thank for creating a place where the experience was possible. Resentment isn't really a bad thing; it came from hurt, a hurt you couldn't experience if you didn't care. Resentment showed you who you are. To be sure, there are more lessons; how many is uncountable. How many lives you live here to define yourself is very individual, but it almost always exceeds one.

HOW DO WE FIX THIS?

We follow the Constitution—the First amendment. We are not a Christian state, we are not a Jewish state, and we are not a Muslim state. We are a secular state by design and purpose, and any other interpretation is given only for self-serving reasons. It isn't valid.

Chapter 11
The Founders

THE CONSTITUTION AND THE BILL OF RIGHTS

In the previous chapters we saw that the intent of the Founders differed greatly from the government we have today. We saw that George Washington was very opposed to political parties and outlined significant reasons for this opposition. We have made it obvious that the political elite's emphasis on security rather than freedom has given them license to scrap the "Bill of Rights" and to step on almost every provision of the Constitution. We have already seen where this is leading us, namely to a police state—just as predicted by George Washington. We have seen that the Wall Street power brokers want to create a worldwide class of politically and economically disenfranchised serfs that will give them absolute control of markets and laws. We have shown that they control the news media so they can direct the news and that all news media, with the possible exception of the internet, is directly controlled by them, and they are attempting to get control of the internet with restrictive legislation.

We have seen that the power brokers on Wall Street use the two political parties to create a false sense of division among Americans, constantly pointing to the superficial rather than substantive issues; therefore, if we face a crisis of the loss of our freedoms under the Constitution, they want the political parties to raise the issue of health care to distract us. If we have a president in the pocket of a foreign power, as Bush was with Saudi Arabia, we create the issue of Obama's birth certificate to keep us divided. If we have rampant unemployment and underemployment, we find foreign wars to keep our focus away from that issue. If Wall Street has completely distorted the economy with worthless debentures and unchecked credit card gouging, we have the mortgage crisis caused by the people who bought homes they couldn't afford, or so says the media, ignoring the hordes of conmen sent out at Wall Street's bidding to get homeowners to convert their stable fixed-term mortgages to adjustable-rate mortgages, which quickly became a burden they couldn't sustain. Nevertheless, according to the corporate media, homeowners caused the economy to collapse, not Wall Street. Of course, each of these diversions is completely supported by the loyal Democrats and Republicans who see their first loyalty to the party and not to their country. Probably Senator Barry Goldwater said it best: "None dare call it treason."

We have examined the foreign policy of the Elitist U.S. government and can find no rationality in it and no obvious cohesion in the actions and statements of this policy. We find ourselves on the wrong side of history by supporting ever more repressive regimes to keep the Wall Street crowd happy. We see that our unconditional support of Israel is a part of this scheme though it has no basis in our values or our legitimate strategic interests. We see the same old attitudes in our educational, scientific, and medical establishments and wonder how educated persons who have reaped the most benefit from this democracy can so easily sell it out for a few bucks.

Lastly, we have looked at the religious institutions that should have been a bulwark against this kind of rampant power hunger, privilege, and greed and discovered a completely incoherent and dysfunctional structure in every major monotheistic religion on Earth. We see the word "hypocrite" emblazoned on their every effort and we find their documented practices of murder, sexual perversion, and political duplicity disgusting.

We live in a society completely upside down compared to the one our Founding Fathers had envisioned for us—a society of the greedy, privileged, and the powerful subverting the disenfranchised citizens and carefully crafted and maintained by the imposition of our two political parties. But it is time to take a very serious look at what they, the Founding Fathers, did have in mind, and see if that is going to fit into the twenty-first century.

In 1787, Alexander Hamilton set his pen to a discourse in the *New York Packet* about the advantages of a union, rather than a confederation of the thirteen former colonies laboring under the Articles of Confederation. His remarks in what we now call *The Federalist Papers* indicate the vision and intention of the Founders. I quote here from Paper 12:

The prosperity of commerce is now perceived and acknowledged by all enlightened statesmen to be the most useful as well as the most productive source of national wealth, and has accordingly become a primary object of their political cares. By multiplying the means of gratification, by promoting the introduction and circulation of the precious metals, those darling objects of human avarice and enterprise, it serves to vivify and invigorate the channels of industry, and to make them flow with greater activity and copiousness. The assiduous merchant, the laborious husbandman, the active mechanic, and the industrious manufacturer,—all orders of men, look forward with eager

expectation and growing alacrity to this pleasing reward of their toils. The often-agitated question between agriculture and commerce has, from indubitable experience, received a decision which has silenced the rivalship that once subsisted between them, and has proved, to the satisfaction of their friends, that their interests are intimately blended and interwoven. It has been found in various countries that, in proportion as commerce has flourished land have risen in value. And how could it have happened otherwise? Could that which procures a freer vent for the products of the earth, which furnishes new incitements to the cultivation of land, which is the most powerful instrument in increasing the quantity of money in a state—could that, in fine, which is the faithful handmaid of labor and industry, in every shape, fail to augment that article, which is the prolific parent of far the greatest part of the objects upon which they are exerted? It is astonishing that so simple a truth should ever have had an adversary; and it is one, among a multitude of proofs, how apt a spirit of ill-informed jealousy, or of too great abstraction and refinement, is to lead men astray from the plainest truths of reason and conviction.

Later in the same article he wrote the following:

What will be the consequence, if we are not able to avail ourselves of the resource in question in its full extent? A nation cannot long exist without revenues. Destitute of this essential support, it must resign its independence, and sink into the degraded condition of a province. This is an extremity to which no government will of choice accede. Revenue, therefore, must be had at all events. In this country, if the principal part be not drawn from commerce, it must fall with oppressive weight upon land. It has been already intimated that excises, in their true signification, are too little in unison with the feelings of the people, to admit of great use being made of that mode of taxation;

nor, indeed, in the States where almost the sole employment is agriculture, are the objects proper for excise sufficiently numerous to permit very ample collections in that way. Personal estate (as has been before remarked), from the difficulty in tracing it, cannot be subjected to large contributions, by any other means than by taxes on consumption. In populous cities, it may be enough the subject of conjecture, to occasion the oppression of individuals, without much aggregate benefit to the State; but beyond these circles, it must, in a great measure, escape the eye and the hand of the tax-gatherer. As the necessities of the State, nevertheless, must be satisfied in some mode or other, the defect of other resources must throw the principal weight of public burdens on the possessors of land. And as, on the other hand, the wants of the government can never obtain an adequate supply, unless all the sources of revenue are open to its demands, the finances of the community, under such embarrassments, cannot be put into a situation consistent with its respectability or its security. Thus we shall not even have the consolations of a full treasury, to atone for the oppression of that valuable class of the citizens who are employed in the cultivation of the soil. But public and private distress will keep pace with each other in gloomy concert; and unite in deploring the infatuation of those counsels which led to disunion.

In Paper 11 he wrote: An unrestrained intercourse between the States themselves will advance the trade of each by an interchange of their respective productions, not only for the supply of reciprocal wants at home, but for exportation to foreign markets. The veins of commerce in every part will be replenished, and will acquire additional motion and vigor from a free circulation of the commodities of every part. Commercial enterprise will have much greater scope, from the diversity in the productions of different States. When the staple of one fails from a bad harvest or unproductive crop, it can call to its aid the staple of another. The variety, not less than the value, of products for exportation contributes to the activity of foreign commerce. It can be conducted upon much better terms with a large number of materials of a given value than with a small number of materials of the same value; arising from the competitions of trade and from the fluctuations of markets. Particular articles may be in great demand at certain periods, and unsalable at others; but if there be a variety of articles, it can scarcely happen that they should all be at one time in the latter predicament, and on this account the operations of the merchant would be less liable to any considerable obstruction or stagnation. The speculative trader will at once perceive the force of these observations, and will acknowledge that the aggregate balance of the commerce of the United States would bid fair to be much more favorable than that of the thirteen States without union or with partial unions.

Americans from the very beginning were keenly interested in the financial rewards the new union would provide, and a lively debate ensued on what and how those advantages would be accrued. But not in a single discourse we have was it envisioned that 1 percent of the population would hold 34 percent of all the wealth and that 20 percent of the population would hold 85 percent of all the wealth, leaving just 15 percent for the other 80 percent of the people. Nothing like that could be imagined in America once we had achieved the goals of our Revolution and so it was not addressed.

"And whither democracy, now that the war had been won?" - Thomas Jefferson 1784

The success of the American experiment was by no means assured in the heady days following the revolution.

Many of the new nation's most important statesmen saw a limited term to the experiment of a democratic republic. John Adams believed that the United States would endure for a century, or maybe for a century and a half. His great-grandson, Henry Adams, later marveled at the audacity of this initial American project to raise the average man on a par with the most favored in terms of intellectual and social opportunity and privilege. He wrote of this radical egalitarianism in his formidable study of American history in the Jeffersonian era:

"The destinies of the United States were certainly staked, without reserve or escape, on the soundness of this doubtful and even improbable principle, ignoring or overthrowing the institutions of the church, aristocracy, family, army and political intervention, which long experience had shown to be needed for the safety of society." – *Henry Adams, The History of the United States of America 1801 - 1817*

Up until now, the improbable principle of egalitarianism, although mitigated, has worked to a fair degree of success in America. For other nations, adventures in democracy have been far more tumultuous.

Over the course of Washington's first administration, two distinct schools of thought began to harden into factions, one led by Hamilton, the other by Jefferson. Because Hamilton's party favored the concentration of federal power, they came to be known as the Federalists. Meanwhile, Jefferson's party, which favored the rights of the states and their constituent members, came to be known as the Democratic-Republicans.

Under Hamilton, the Federalist platform held that the United States needed to expand its centralized powers by taking a loose constructionist view of the Constitution. By this approach, the federal government reserved the right to

227

pursue all action and legislation not expressly denied to it in the Constitution. In support of their view, they cited the so-called elastic clause of the Constitution (Article I, Section 8), which provides the federal government with the power to make all laws "which shall be necessary and proper for the successful furtherance of the nation." At the time, such initiatives included the establishment of a national bank, the encouragement of industry, and the furtherance of an autonomous economy. Pro-alliance, the Federalists tended to reserve their sympathies in foreign affairs for the British.

Meanwhile, the Democratic-Republicans furthered a strict constructionist view of the Constitution, by which the federal government enjoyed only those powers expressly delegated to it in the Constitution. To support their view, they pointed to the Tenth Amendment in the Bill of Rights, which states that the powers not delegated to the United States...are reserved to the states respectively, or to the people. Thus, the Democratic-Republicans, in support of individual rights and distrustful of king-making policies, opposed the strongly nationalistic measures of the Federalists. In addition, under Jefferson they emphasized the role of agrarian America at the expense of industrialization and encouraged free trade over political alliance. Insofar as the Democratic-Republicans had an ally, it was France, which was in the process of enacting its own radical egalitarian reforms, to mixed and often bloody success.

In this early political divide lies the key to much of America's succeeding political heritage. The first spate of name-calling was propagated by Hamilton and Jefferson: Jefferson characterized Hamilton as the architect of a tissue of machinations against the liberty of the country; Hamilton pithily assessed Jefferson as a contemptible hypocrite. Regional differences also began to emerge more clearly in this difficult era. Out of loyalty to New York, Hamilton looked to foster the interests of big business and industry and wished to establish a strong financial base. Jefferson's loyalty to Virginia manifested itself in his devotion to agricultural interests, free trade, and state's rights. All of these issues would remain contentious sores on the face of national unity until they gradually drove the union asunder and into civil war.

The political challenge has always been to steer the difficult middle course between the potential tyranny of Hamilton's system and the potential anarchy of Jefferson's system. The greatest irony of all was that Jefferson, the well-born aristocrat, believed in government by the people, and that Hamilton, the illegitimate son of an island tryst, believed in government by a elite. Such reversals are also a part of America's political legacy: consider the liberality of the high-toned Franklin D. Roosevelt and the conservatism of the down-home Ronald Reagan.

Whereas Washington trusted Jefferson in matters of foreign policy, he tended to follow Hamilton more closely with regard to domestic affairs. Again, the pattern resurfaces even today, as the United States tends to take a Jeffersonian approach to free trade while assuming a Hamiltonian stance in regard to finance. While Jefferson is revered as the more favored statesman, Hamilton made an equally significant imprint on the character of the federal government during these formative years under Washington.

As Hamilton and Jefferson continued to bicker publicly, Washington's first term drew to a close. To understand Washington it is useful to go back in time to a period before the Revolution had begun and get his opinion on the governance of the British Crown.

At a time, when our lordly masters in Great Britain will be satisfied with nothing less than the deprivation of American freedom, it seems highly necessary that something should

be done to avert the stroke, and maintain the liberty, which we have from our ancestors. But the manner of doing it, to answer the purpose effectually, is the point in question. That no man should scruple, or hesitate a moment, to use arms in defense of so valuable a blessing, on which all the good and evil of life depends, is clearly my opinion. Yet arms, I would beg leave to add, should be the last resource, the dernier resort. Addresses to the throne, and remonstrance's to Parliament, we have already, it is said, proved the inefficacy of. How far, then, their attention to our rights and privileges is to be awakened or alarmed, by starving their and , remains to be tried. —George Washington, letter to George Mason, April 5, 1769

It is clear Washington was well done with the British and the Crown long before the Declaration of Independence, and would have taken up arms against them at the drop of a hat. But he chose to try economic sanctions first, just as our modern presidents have done. But then like now these are ineffective because the root cause, the issue, is not economics, but power.

The good dispositions which seem at present to pervade every class of people afford reason for your observation that the clouds which have long darkened our political hemisphere are now dispersing, and that America will soon feel the effects of her natural advantages. That invisible hand which has so often interposed to save our Country from impending destruction, seems in no instance to have been more remarkably excited than in that of disposing the people of this extensive to adopt, in a peaceable manner, a Constitution, which if well administered, bids fair to make America a happy nation. —George Washington, letter to Philip Schuyler, May 9, 1789

As he started his first term in office we can see Washington's optimistic side emerge and that he felt that all of his endeavors to secure that Country which he now led were worthwhile. But after eight years of governing and experiencing the pressures of disunity and divided loyalties, he had much to advise his new nation about as he wrote his farewell address:

It is important, likewise, that the habits of thinking in a free country should inspire caution in those entrusted with its administration, to confine themselves within their respective constitutional spheres, avoiding in the exercise of the powers of one department to encroach upon another. The spirit of encroachment tends to the powers of all the departments in one, and thus to create, whatever the form of government, a real despotism. A just estimate of that love of power, and proneness to abuse it, which predominates in the human heart, is sufficient to satisfy us of the truth of this position. The necessity of reciprocal checks in the exercise of political power, by dividing and distributing it into different depositaries, and constituting each the guardian of the public weal against invasions by the others, has been evinced by experiments ancient and modern; some of them in our country and under our own eyes. To preserve them must be as necessary as to institute them. If, in the opinion of the people, the distribution or modification of the constitutional powers be in any particular wrong, let it be corrected by an amendment in the way which the Constitution designates. But let there be no change by usurpation; for though this, in one instance, may be the instrument of good, it is the customary weapon by which free governments are destroyed. The precedent must always greatly overbalance in permanent evil any partial or transient benefit, which the use can at any time yield.

Note the caution to say "let there be no change by usurpation," exactly the precedent that Bush and Chaney were successful in pulling off and, for that matter, the precedent that Franklin Roosevelt succeeded in pulling off. Each used the common denominator of war to excuse the usurpation. Both will clearly be denigrated by history for it.

The poor people, it is true, have been much less successful than the great. They have seldom found either leisure or opportunity to form a union and exert their strength; ignorant as they were of arts and letters, they have seldom been able to frame and support a regular opposition. This, however, has been known by the great to be the temper of mankind; and they have accordingly labored, in all ages, to wrest from the populace, as they are contemptuously called, the knowledge of their rights and wrongs, and the power to assert the former or redress the latter. I say RIGHTS, for such they have, undoubtedly, antecedent to all earthly government,—Rights, that cannot be repealed or restrained by human laws - Rights, derived from the great Legislator of the universe. —John Adams, A Dissertation on the Canon and Feudal Law, 1765

The basis of our political systems is the right of the people to make and to alter their Constitutions of Government. But the Constitution which at any time exists, till changed by an explicit and authentic act of the whole people, is sacredly obligatory upon all. The very idea of the power and the right of the people to establish Government presupposes the duty of every individual to obey the established Government. — George Washington, Farewell Address, September 19, 1796

If Washington still lived, his calls for changes to the Constitution to stop the Political-Financial Complex would be uniting us to do battle with this awful usurpation of the rights of the people.

As a very important source of strength and security, cherish public credit. One method of preserving it is, to use it as sparingly as possible; avoiding occasions of by cultivat-

ing peace, but remembering also that timely disbursements to prepare for danger frequently prevent much greater disbursements to repel it; avoiding likewise the accumulation of debt, not only by shunning occasions of expense, but by vigorous exertions in time of peace to discharge , which unavoidable wars may have occasioned, not ungenerously throwing upon posterity the burden, which we ourselves ought to bear. —George Washington, Farewell Address, September 19, 1796

I think this statement demonstrates that our first president was opposed to creating enormous government debt. No doubt he would be joining the chorus of voices who say we cannot sustain this callous disregard for sound economic principles and hope to survive. No doubt he would support the imposition of a balanced budget amendment.

Observe good faith and justice towards all Nations; cultivate peace and with all. Religion and Morality enjoin this conduct; and can it be that good policy does not equally enjoin it? It will be worthy of a free, enlightened, and, at no distant period, a great Nation, to give to mankind the magnanimous and too novel example of a people always guided by an exalted justice and benevolence. Who can doubt, that, in the course of time and things, the fruits of such a plan would richly repay any temporary advantages, which might be lost by a steady adherence to it? Can it be, that Providence has not the permanent felicity of a Nation with its Virtue? —George Washington, Farewell Address, September 19, 1796

Again, we see that our government has gone completely in the opposite direction from its Founders hoped for; that we have a foreign policy promoting despotism abroad and aligning ourselves with the aspirations of a domineering European colonialism is completely backward to our original direction—a direction we were able to maintain through our first five presidencies. We are the despot, the oppressor, and the power-hungry Elitist that we so vehemently opposed in our Revolution. Oh how the wheel turns. Please pay attention to Washington's last question in the above quote and ask yourself where we might find our nation's fortunes in the near future. Yet our Founding Father, held a great respect for, and trust in, the people of his country to do the right thing and to continue the traditions and the principles of a free people; to nurture and cultivate the Tree of Liberty, and bring forth a great change for all of humanity.

As for myself I am now seated in the shade of my Vine and Fig tree, and altho' I look with regret on many transactions which do not comport with my ideas, I shall, notwithstanding "view them in the calm lights of mild philosophy," persuaded, if any great crisis should occur, to require it, that the good sense and Spirit of the Major part of the people of this country, will direct them properly. —George Washington, letter to Charles Cotesworth Pinckney, June 24, 1797

The great mass of our citizens require only to understand matters rightly, to form right decisions. —George Washington, letter to James Lloyd, February 11, 1799

And Washington was not alone in his sentiments about the character of his people and the outcome for his nation.

But what do we mean by the American Revolution? Do we mean the American war? The Revolution was effected before the war commenced. The Revolution was in the minds and hearts of the people; a change in their religious sentiments, of their duties and obligations... This radical change in the principles, opinions, sentiments, and affections of the people was the real American Revolution. — John Adams, letter to H. Niles, February 13, 1818

If you think everything was settled and that our first president had smooth sailing during his two terms, read this:

It is with equal pride and satisfaction I add, that as far as my information extends, this insurrection is viewed with universal indignation and abhorrence; except by those who have never missed an opportunity by side blows, or otherwise, to aim their shafts at the general government; and even among these there is not a Spirit hardy enough, yet, openly to justify the daring infractions of Law and order; but by palliatives are attempting to suspend all proceedings against the insurgents until Congress shall have decided on the case, thereby intending to gain time, and if possible to make the evil more extensive, more formidable, and of course more difficult to counteract and subdue. I consider this insurrection as the first formidable fruit of the Democratic Societies; brought forth I believe too prematurely for their own views, which may contribute to the annihilation of them. That these societies were instituted by the artful and designing members (many of their body I have no doubt mean well, but know little of the real plan,) primarily to sow the seeds of jealousy and distrust among the people, of the government, by destroying all confidence in the Administration of it; and that these doctrines have been budding and blowing ever since, is not new to anyone, who is acquainted with the characters of their leaders, and has been attentive to their maneuvers. I early gave it as my opinion to the confidential characters around me, that, if these Societies were not counteracted (not by prosecutions, the ready way to make them grow stronger) or did not fall into disesteem from the knowledge of their origin, and the views with which they had been instituted by their father, Genet, for purposes well known to the Government; that they would shake the government to its foundation.

Time and circumstances have confirmed me in this opinion, and I deeply regret the probable consequences, not as they will affect me personally, (for I have not long to act on this theatre, and sure I am that not a man amongst them can be more anxious to put me aside, than I am to sink into the profoundest retirement) but because I see, under a display of popular and fascinating guises, the most diabolical attempts to destroy the best fabric of human government and happiness, that has ever been presented for the acceptance of mankind. —George Washington, letter to Richard Henry Lee, August 22, 1794

During 1793 and 1794, a series of explosive controversies divided followers of Hamilton and Jefferson. Washington's administration confronted a French effort to entangle the United States in its war with England, armed rebellion in western Pennsylvania, Indian resistance, and the threat of another war with Britain. These controversies intensified party spirit and increased voting along party lines in Congress.

In April 1793, "Citizen" Edmond Charles Genet (1763–1834), a French minister, arrived in the United States and passed out letters authorizing Americans to attack British commercial vessels and Spanish New Orleans. Washington regarded these actions as a clear violation of American neutrality and demanded that France recall its minister. The Genet affair had an important effect—it intensified party feeling. From Vermont to South Carolina citizens organized Democratic-Republican clubs to celebrate the triumphs of the French Revolution. Hamilton and his supporters suspected that these societies really existed to stir up grassroots opposition to the Washington administration. The seeds of disunity were planted, and we have yet to pull the weeds.

Below we see what one of the Founders, Benjamin Franklin, thought would be the deportment of Congress under the new Constitution. Little did he know that they would use the power of lawmaking and the purse strings to enrich themselves to the detriment of their fellow citizens and to turn his idealism into a triumph of despotism. More to the point he could not have anticipated the rise of the professional politician, it was not imagined that anyone would want to do the dirty work of government for a living. As we now know if you let them continue in the position they will turn it into a source of great wealth for themselves and their sponsors; and they will add all the privilege the country can muster to the benefit of their self aggrandizement.

They are of the People, and return again to mix with the People, having no more durable preeminence than the different Grains of Sand in an Hourglass. Such an Assembly cannot easily become dangerous to Liberty. They are the Servants of the People, sent together to do the People's , and promote the public Welfare; their Powers must be sufficient, or their Duties cannot be performed. They have no profitable Appointments, but a mere of daily Wages, such as are scarcely equivalent to their Expenses; so that, having no Chance for great Places, and enormous Salaries or Pensions, as in some Countries, there is no triguing or bribing for Elections. Benjamin Franklin, letter to George Whatley, May 23, 1785.

It is our hope that you now see the intention of our Founding Fathers; it had nothing to do with Wall Street, with Elitist political parties, with oligarchical multinational industries, or with unsustainable economic and military adventurism. It was simple, down-to-earth, and egalitarian. The Founders could not have imagined where this might lead, but they trusted in the people to maintain it. Unfortunately in the past forty to fifty years that trust has been misplaced, but we still can turn this around and we still can unite this country as one people to one purpose. We can never do that with our current political parties. We cannot do it with our elitist governmental agencies, our elitist courts, and our puppet masters in New York City.

Before we conclude our history review, though, we must examine the Civil War. The Civil War was fought to right a tremendous wrong, slavery, and it was brewing from the very first day the thirteen states came together in a union. It established once and for all that we are all equal, we are all endowed with certain inalienable rights, and we have the right to pursue happiness. Become aware of how you are being manipulate by the Elite to divide us and control us when you buy into the raciest idea; it results in some of the stupidest voting patterns on Earth. This is the problem and it will remain the problem until you learn what you have actually inherited and what potential you throw away every time you go to the voting booth. If you are sitting up at night on some distant battlefield waiting for an enemy attack and the guy in the next foxhole, or right beside you, is black, red, yellow, brown, or white and you still don't know who your brother is, you are a moron. Your bother is the one who stands beside you and fights with you for your freedom and for your children's freedom, and no more brother will you ever have. You are not living in the country your forefathers fought for you to have; you are living in a nightmare of manipulation and division that would destroy any people or nation. All of it created by the Elite who you still vote for and allow to ruin your lives. You have only yourself to blame for it, donkey.

HOW DO WE FIX THIS?

Let me start out by asking you if you know what America will be like in two hundred years. Do you know what our transportation will look like? Do you know what fashion will be in vogue? Do you have any idea what kind of jobs we will have? Do you understand the science we will understand or the technology we will invent? Do you know how we will live? Of course you don't. Neither did our Founding Fathers fully anticipate what today would look like, but they, like us, cared about what we would become. Therefore, the Constitution is designed to be amended, and amend it, we must. We must have an amendment outlawing lobbying. We must have an amendment mandating a balanced budget. We must have an amendment forbidding any president or Congress from starting a war without the consent of the governed. We must have an amendment that prohibits any U.S. government from contributing to the defense or the establishment of a dictatorial regime anywhere in the world, or having close diplomatic relations or trade with a totalitarian regime. This must include those states that deny women their rights, have archaic rule by a monarchy, or insist on telling their citizens what religion they must follow.

We must have an amendment limiting terms for Supreme Court justices, for all federal judgeships, and for members of Congress. We must have an amendment that says specifically that corporations are not citizens and they cannot engage in executing any of the rights and privileges of a citizen on penalty of their board members and executives being arrested and put in jail. We must have an amendment that says if you are not an American registered company you cannot do business in this country and you cannot contribute to any political party or movement. We must have an amendment that says any government official accepting a gift of money or other valuable gift from a foreign entity will be charged with official misconduct or impeached.

We must have an amendment that prohibits ownership of any media, be it print, radio, television, or internet, by any foreign entity and it must limit ownership by American citizens to just one such media outlet. Finally, to stop speculators and the damage they do to stable prices, we need an amendment making it a crime to operate any bank, service, or entity that allows its member or nonmembers to bid on the price of securities or commodities. And in this amendment we shut down for good the New York Stock Exchange and the Chicago Board of Trade.

Chapter 12
The Pursuit of Happiness

"But with respect to future debt; would it not be wise and just for that nation to declare in the constitution they are forming that neither the legislature, nor the nation itself can validly contract more debt, than they may pay within their own age, or within the term of 19 years."**
—Thomas Jefferson, September 6, 1789

HOW DO WE FIX THIS?

As disturbing as all of this seems, as abysmal as it has become for the American Middle Class, it is not beyond our capability to correct these errors. The Constitution of the United States of America has remedies for all of these excesses. That is where we begin. To be sure, the two current political parties are not going to give up power without a fight. The citizens, the electorate, can expect that any and all attempt to create a level playing field for the American Middle Class, 80 percent of the population, will be met with every kind of resistance. Of course, the first kind of resistance will be their old standby —the misinformation campaigns—divide and conquer. The Wall Street kingmakers, the two political parties, the multinational corporations, and the media will fight everything offered, so be aware that a propaganda campaign will take up all of commercial television and all of the available radio transmissions to debunk and to deride any effort at reform.

But some things must change, or change will come in an out-of-control manner that even the Elite will find hard to take advantage of. The unsustainable growth in our economy is the first place it has to stop. Constant inflation, fueled by the need for ever greater returns on investment, must come to an end. We are trashing the planet, and soon it will be unlivable. This is not the usual environmental concern; it is simply a fact. We will be out of oil by 2030 (at least any oil we can afford), we will be out of fish by 2045, fresh water by 2065, and arable land by 2090. Population growth to fuel the consumer economy will be unsustainable by 2060, when literally more people will die than are born because of malnutrition, disease, and lack of shelter. The Wall Street model of ever expanding markets is a pipe dream and will cause more grief than the Inquisition, the two world wars, and international jihad combined.

We have to start simple, but hit at the greatest abuses. The first target has to be the lobbyists on K Street. We must create a Constitutional amendment outlawing lobbying of any kind. The second target has to be the influence of money in the election process; we need a Constitutional amendment to outlaw corporations from contributing money to anything political, and it must specifically say that corporations are not citizens and do not have any right of citizenship—only people can be citizens. The third target has to be the diversification of the media. We need a Constitutional amendment that will not allow any person, corporation, or group of people or entities from owning more than one television station, one radio station, or one newspaper; they cannot own any more than one of these separately or individually. Without diversity we go back to the managed corporate news that got us here in the first place—the so-called politically correct news. The fourth target has to be the restrictive laws that govern who can register as a political party and who is allowed access to the ballots. True democracy requires unrestricted access for the citizens to the elective process. In fact, in keeping with the Founding Father's preferences, the amendment must say that any citizen can be represented on a ballot, not just a political party.

Now we need some more radical reforms that will enthrone the Middle Class in the position of power ever afterward. The first of these is the right, not the privilege, of having a job. A law like this was discussed in 1946 when the soldiers came home from World War II, but it was not enacted. We need this as part of a Constitutional guarantee. This amendment is not a requirement that you work—if you choose not to be employed, that is your business—but it is a guarantee that if you want a job, a job will be given to you. The social benefits of this for the family unit cannot be overestimated, and the reduction in crime and the cost of incarceration will more than offset the cost of providing jobs to all who want to work. This is quite simply a right—it is not a privilege. Men and women are made to work; we must have the sense of contribution to our communities and the sense of purpose that work allows. Without it we are never going to be what we are here to be. It is not the right of any government or financial agency to deny our right to work. We have way more than enough work to do; look at the lasting legacy of the CCC and WPA, we can use every willing worker to rebuild infrastructure, maintain our forests, and protect our national parks. This time around though, we need a new vision and a new purpose for this work program. The new vision is that it is a cooperative effort of community's first, states second and national government third. It is not a mandate from the national government, it is a community based effort with businesses and all community service agencies involved. The money comes from the budgets we have trimmed away from the Elite that don't go for corporate wars and bailouts. We keep that money in our communities by reducing the federal income tax burden to zero. That's right we repeal the 16th amendment. We then have money in our communities' not in Washington and we use it to get community priorities accomplished. Maybe the dumbest thing we do is to keep an unemployed person on government unemployment assist while we let their work skills deteriorate and make them unemployable. All we do is waste our money doing that. Why not have a trained and ready workforce doing productive things for our communities instead of a wasted workforce sitting ideally while their skills deteriorate and they lose hope. Is there really a choice to make in this situation? How dumb do you have to be to do it the way our Elite are doing it now? Then they say we have to compete in a global economy while they waste the best resource we have – our people.

Then we need reform of the financial houses themselves; we must restore a national usury law to stop the gouging, and we need laws that make it a crime to invest money in anything that does not enhance commercial and industry development. After that we must have a Constitutional amendment that requires Congress to balance the budget. The same amendment must also require Congress to *develop* the budget—no more having the president present the budget. The Constitution is very specific about this requirement, and it does not have the executive branch supply the budget to the legislative branch. Congress needs to do this itself. The main reason they need to do this is because they will no longer be voting on the budget: that will be done by national referendum on a section by section basis. If some sections get voted down, then Congress has to go back to work and revise them and present them again for citizen approval. So the work of the Congress is changed from power brokering the provisions of the budget to preparing the budget—not as glamorous, but certainly needed. The people decide on the budget and the president does not stick his nose into it—by law.

Of course we will need many sessions of Congress to repeal laws; the stridently privileged laws made for the elite classes that now exist all must go. By now I think you have realized that all of this will not get done with any dispatch unless we handle it altogether as a package. Again, the Constitution has a remedy for that. It is just amazing how far-sighted our Founders were. We will have to hold a Constitutional Convention, as discussed in Article. V.

The Congress, whenever two thirds of both Houses shall deem it necessary, shall propose Amendments to this Constitution, or, on the Application of the Legislatures of two thirds of the several States, shall call a Convention for proposing Amendments, which, in either Case, shall be valid to all Intents and Purposes, as Part of this Constitution, when ratified by the Legislatures of three fourths of the several States, or by Conventions in three fourths thereof, as the one or the other Mode of Ratification may be proposed by the Congress...

Finally, and most importantly, we need a statement in our Constitution that under no circumstances and in no foreseeable situation will the Bill of Rights or any provision in the Bill of Rights be suspended. Asking our youth to go fight and die for a Constitution that has been suspended is absurd. Our youth in the armed forces do not make allegiance to a man or a congress; they make their allegiance to the Constitution. They do not make allegiance to a political party or a president; they are making an oath to protect and defend the Constitution. For a politician to suspend that very document that people are pledged to defend is like everything else these two political parties touch—completely upside down and backwards. This has to be stopped with an amendment to make it unconstitutional under penalty of prosecution for treason.

If we refuse to vote for either a Republican or a Democratic candidate and we put in place representatives in the various state legislatures who are committed to holding a Constitutional Convention, we will see in our lifetimes a complete reversal of our political structure and the elimination of the elite aristocracy we have grown to resent, despise, and abhor as a free people. We have endured their excesses too long. We have distorted our American values too long. We have disappointed those in the rest of the world longing for us to take up the mantle of freedom too long. We must become Americans again; we are not Democrats and Republicans—we are Americans. I would add that we also need to look at how we can restore our honor as a nation. That bunch of 19th century Robber Barons took everything they could get their greedy little hands on, including almost all of the Native American lands agreed to by treaty between the tribes and the government of the United States. These treaties were ratified by Congress. For the sake of Wall Street greed we broke everyone of them. We need to restore our honor as a people by returning the Black Hills to the tribes we agreed would own it. We need to look at the many other sites that have been similarly stolen and return them to the rightful owners. A lot of these sites are as sacred to Native Americans as Jerusalem is to the three monotheistic religions. Our honor demands we return them to the people we stole them from.

Once we regain our constitutional republic and we wrest control from Wall Street and give it back to Main

Street what will we have accomplished? We will still have 20 percent holding 85 percent of all the wealth of this nation, rampant poverty in a nation supposed to be the richest on Earth, and an unsustainable economic system based on a consumer economy disintegrating before our eyes. So we will have corrected the political path, but we also must correct the economic path.

We cannot correct our economy so long as we follow the corporate model, a model that says that the economic value of a business entity is due solely to the capital invested in it by the investor class and the reason for the existence of a corporation is to make sure that investor is paid back and makes a handsome profit to boot. He did, after all, take all that risk. This model is not working and its premise is not correct. The investor on Wall Street is not a risk taker, unlike those "angel investors" I mentioned earlier; he is trying to maximize his gain against the ebb and flow of the economy—he is risk adverse. So why it is the paramount concern of every corporate entity on Earth to be sure the investor is happy? This is because they risk losing a source of funding if he isn't happy, but this fear is also based on a faulty premise; if they are doing well and showing profits, he will invest—if not, he won't. So where is the advantage of catering to investors? If your company is failing, the Wall Street investor is the last person on Earth who will lend you money. If your company is succeeding, he will jump onboard and drive up your stock price to get in on the *speculative* prospect of your venture. He really doesn't know what you do or how you do it; all he wants is the opportunity to speculate on your success. So we really don't have investors on Wall Street: we have speculators. What good does that do for anyone but them? That, by definition, gives us a nation whose sole purpose in existence is to allow speculators to exploit every business entity they can to make profits for themselves. I'm sorry, but I miss the socially redeeming aspect of this scenario. I must just be un-American.

What if the purpose of economic activity were to make all citizens economically strong and free of corrupt oppression? Would that make a difference? How would we do that? Might I suggest we change the structure of corporations as we now know them? Instead of being driven by the intentions of speculators, we will make them entities devoted to providing economic advantage to their employees, after all the employees of any business have made an investment in the success of that business with their labor and their intellect, why wouldn't they receive the return on their investment just like the person who invested his money? Now that is what I call an incentive plan. But it has to come with a fundamental change in our psyche. We can *all* enjoy the wonderful benefits of the system of governance our forefathers gave us, not just the few. We can all know our lives to be in our control, not in the control of the greedy, the state, or the multinational corporations, but ours. We have this opportunity and we have the legal apparatus to achieve it.Right now we have business entities set up to accomplish this end. They are known as "mutual" companies. The concept is that the persons served by these entities are the owners of the entity and they have a share in its success. I would suggest we take that idea and apply it to the workplace, the new business model for a true democracy. The employees become the mutual owners of the company. They are, after all is said and done, the ones who will make or break the company, and they are the natural inheritors of its success or failure. They are the ones who actually know what the company is doing, why it exists, and what it hopes to accomplish. Wall Street speculators just don't know that or understand it. Why then wouldn't the employees be the ones who experience the fruit of their labors, not some speculator who is risk adverse to start with? A mutual company will, in fact, out compete and out innovate any other model, precisely because the employees will have the drive to see it succeed and to want it to outperform all their competition. They will only have that drive if the rewards come to them, however, not some speculator on Wall Street. Real investors will see this and know it will quickly return their investment and will give them rewards for a long time. This model just doesn't work for multinational companies that are spread all over the globe because the employees never form a bond and never experience the trust and confidence that their efforts will be rewarded. Mutual entities are best when they serve a specific community and use their assets and profits to enrich that community. From this model we can make the egalitarian dreams of our forefathers come to life, and we will restore our freedoms with it. The American Middle Class will again own their country and their dreams.

Consider that our current system has given away hundreds of billions, if not trillions, of dollars to other countries who are run by despotic regimes who hold their citizens in a grip of despair and poverty that only the kings and royalty could have managed in the prior world of aristocratic control. We did this while making more than three quarters of the world community hate us. They hate us because they rightly conclude that their oppressors could not succeed without our help. They see us as the new colonial power trying to tell everyone how to live and what to think, and they are not wrong about us. But consider what America might have been if we had not followed the path of globalization, the Wal-Mart economy, police state mentality, and constant warfare to maintain the economic advantages of multinational corporations who want to enslave us.

One of the best ways to understand where you are at and how you got there is to step back and try to see what might have been the outcome if you made different decisions along the way. Let's go back to 1947. The Congress of the United States has recently voted to join the United Nations and is now considering a bill that would guarantee a job to any citizen who is seeking employment in the country. It is being considered because we have so much gratitude for the valiant efforts made by our citizens in uniform over the course of the recently concluded World War II. In this same year President Harry Truman will make the United States the first nation to recognize the newly created state of Israel. So the year 1947 saw America make some momentous decisions about the direction the country would take and the resultant future we would experience together. It was a watershed year. Where would we be if each of these decisions made differently?

First we would not belong to the United Nations as Eleanor Roosevelt wanted us to, and we would not have been able to sell the citizenry on the idea of globalization if we didn't belong, for two reasons: (1) the United Nations would probably have failed without us, and (2) the idea of involving ourselves in efforts to diminish our economy by giving away our industrial advantages would not have had any political wings behind it. Without globalization Sam Walton doesn't have the political backing to undermine our entire industrial infrastructure so he can make a buck. Plus there is another thing he doesn't have: he doesn't have the cheap, downtrodden workforce he needs to undermine the mom-and-pop stores and put his big boxes all over the country because we passed the jobs-guarantee bill and everyone has a job who wants one. Cheap labor is a thing that doesn't exist here.

We would undoubtedly have gone down the road of the Cold War with or without the UN, but without it we would have made more decisive and more nationally appropriate decisions instead of the weak and wimpy decisions we made that often violated our American values. An example of that would be the way the UN soldiers handled the Rwanda massacre or the years and lives wasted in Bosnia without political or military leadership to resolve the problem. Therefore our Cold War isn't going to last as long or to have such long-lasting repercussions. Problems like the tumult in Bosnia are fixed much more quickly, if we are involved at all—and that is doubtful. As for Israel, we recognize her, but we insist she pay reparations and she negotiate with her neighbors. The Europeans will, for sure, recognize her; they have a hefty guilty conscious. Her real survival and her real acceptance are doubtful, but not impossible. Israel politicians would have to become diplomats instead of warlords; they would actually have to negotiate for their future instead of having a superpower to back them up, which would make for quite a difference. I doubt they would have become part of the proliferating nuclear bomb problem that they are now. I do believe that the problem of continuing unsettled Palestinian issues would have long since been settled. For both Israel and the United States this relationship has been one of lose-lose, not win-win.

With no ongoing Israeli problem, most of the wars we have fought in the Middle East and North Africa would never have occurred. Our relations with the Arab world would be a lot more commercial, and a lot less political. We would certainly still have the Wahhabis in Saudi Arabia, but if we refused to do business with countries that deny women their rights how long would they last? We would certainly be buying oil from someplace for a while longer until we get the green economy going it just wouldn't be from them. We would not be so easy a target for the Wahhabis to demonize and make their Great Satan. No doubt someone else would be though, just not us. It is also doubtful that we would have engaged in the first or second gulf war, and without us, it just wouldn't happen. So a lot of things would change if we could just go back to 1947. Almost all of them would be beneficial, not to Wall Street—but to the American Middle Class.

It is important to understand that all of these decisions, which would never have been made by our Founders, are still reversible. We can still opt out of the UN, and we can stop supporting Israel against all reason and thought and treat her like any other small country bent on religious exclusivism, much like our relations with Bhutan, Eritrea, or Armenia today. We can pass the law to guarantee jobs to all who want them. But we have only scratched the surface of what-ifs when we reverse these disastrous decisions. A vote in Congress to actually guarantee the jobs of all American citizens would have been as revolutionary as any ever taken in our Congress, including the vote to ratify the Constitution itself. The outcome would be an America we cannot imagine today. It would have completely changed the emphasis in the government from one of making American business strong to making American families strong. If that emphasis had shifted, would we have the economy we are dealing with today? Would poverty and lack of parental involvement have led us to a society that has constant drive-by shootings in every major city in the country? Without abject poverty and laws that constantly played against the family to the benefit of the corporations, would we have the crime, prisons, and lack of community unity we have today? Would half our children be raised in single-parent situations, if poverty did not destroy the family unit with debt and broken dreams? Would we allow our children to grow up in ghettos without any after-school sports, without any Boy/Girl Scouts, without any adult supervision? Would we see the kind of school systems we have, or would we have real competition among schools for the betterment of our children? We won't know until we try.

I hear the Republicans now: you can't guarantee jobs for everyone; we can't afford to support that—it will bankrupt the government! This is nonsense, and they know it. If we actually had a full-employment economy, we would have such an explosion in opportunity and small businesses that we could not keep up. I didn't say the people who got jobs would stop paying taxes; I said we would guarantee that job. I didn't say it would be in the government sector: it certainly could be in the private sector. Just like the government guarantees loans for students or housing loans for veterans, it could guarantee jobs for the unemployed. Why pay someone to sit for thirty-nine months as they do now, never knowing whether they can return to the class of working citizens who pay taxes, when you could have their labor and stop a recession in its tracks. That is just stupid, but that is how Wall Street puppet representatives think—stupid. They are so class-conscious that they don't realize that creating a sustained economy without major downturns is possible and practical and will cost less in the long run than the cycle of boom and bust that Wall Street loves. It will cost less in the long run also if we stop fighting foreign wars for the sake of multinational corporations, stop supporting despots, and start applying a foreign policy that actually helps Americans. We can only guess at the social benefits of that system. Of course it won't work if we maintain the constant flow of illegal immigration that has characterized the period since 1947. That is allowed to provide cheap labor for Wall Street firms and to undermine the wage structure of American workers so we can keep the inequities of the system that lets them live like kings on our backs. Do you really think we couldn't close our borders? To quote a recent president, "Yes we can."

Once we take Wall Street out of Washington and go back to a government of the people, by the people, and for the people; we will reap enormous advantages. We will end the boom or bust cycle, we will stop fighting ridiculous wars, we will strengthen our family units, and we will see the blight of poverty disappear from our towns and cities. In short the pursuit of happiness will again have meaning. The real question is why have we settled for less for so long? You tell me, donkey!

Ok donkeys, here is a list for each of you that will turn you from donkeys to citizens of the Greatest Country on Earth.

- Refuse to vote for or support any Republican or Democratic candidate in local, state or national government elections.

- Get your voice heard, get on the internet, put it on face-book, blog your concerns, and get others to do the same. Get a movement started.

- Start organizing a grassroots movement at the local level, not by doing a sit in at the local park, but by renting a hall and inviting people to a real community meeting to overthrow the Elite wherever you live. Remember the freedom and happiness of your children are at stake, fight for them to have a better future.

- In your voting and in your thought process think of community first, community first in our schools, community first in our health care, community first in the ownership of our news media, community first in our police forces, community first in our employment and job opportunities. The Elite have proven to all of us over and over again they cannot govern from Washington or anywhere else. We must have community control of our lives.

- Question your government, don't be seeking their favor, make them seek your favor. Why are we supporting foreign dictators, why do they think it necessary to suspend our Constitutional rights so they can fight wars for the benefit of multinational corporations, why do we have money for Wall Street bailouts, but no money to help home owners keep their homes, etc? Don't let them get away with it.

- Demand that your news media be free from corporate shackles. Demand that foreign influences are not allowed to control our news media. Don't buy, listen to, or watch multinational corporate owned news media.

- Insist that the elections at all levels be free of restrictive laws, gerrymandering, and filing fees that allow the Republicans and Democrats control the outcome of elections.

- Finally use your buying power to punish corporate greed in both retail and in your investments. With hold your purchases from those who lobby to restrain your freedoms and to tilt the playing field in their favor.

Reference Section

Hamilton, Alexander; Madison, James; Jay, John; *The Federalist Papers*, Philadelphia, PA, The new American Library, April 1961

Ketcham, Ralph; *The Anti-Federalist Papers*, New York, NY, Penguin Group, October 1986

De Tocqueville, Alexis; *Democracy in America*, New York, NY, Vintage Books, September 1954

Unger, Craig; *House of Bush House of Saud*, New York, NY, Scribner, March 2004

Johnston, David Cay; *New York Times - Gap between rich, poor widens*, New York, NY, New York Times, March 29, 2007

Edward N. Wolff at New York University (2010); *Recent Trends in Household Wealth in the United States: Rising Debt and the Middle-Class Squeeze*, New York, NY, June, 2007.

Wright, Robert E and Cowan, David J.; *Financial Founding Fathers, The Men Who Made America Rich*, University of Chicago Press, May 2006

Blanchette, Claude; *Public and private Sector Involvement in Health Care System, Bulletin 438E,* London, UK, Library of Parliament, November, 1997.

The Physicians for Human Rights (PHR) report, *Experiments in Torture: Human Subject Research and Evidence of Experimentation in the 'Enhanced' Interrogation Program, 2010*

Chantrill, Christopher: *Spending on Education,* usgovernmentspending.com , 2011

Organization for Education Cooperation and Development (OECD), *Student assessments,* 2009

Mullins, Eustace: *The Secrets of the Federal Reserve,* Bankers Research Institute, Staunton, VA.,1993

Table References

Table 1: Distribution of Net Worth and Financial Wealth in the United States, Page 23 (Wolff 2010)

Table 2: Wealth Distribution by Type of Asset, Page 26 (Wolff 2007)

Table 3: Wealth Distribution by Type of Other Asset, Page 27 (Wolff 2007)

Table 4: Annual Average Changes in Productivity and Related Measures (2006-2010), Page 30(US Bureau of Labor Statistics)

Table 5: Manufacturing Productivity (2007-2008), Page 32 [International Comparison of Productivity and Unit Labor Cost Trends (2008)]

Table 6: Disposable Personal Income, Page 57, U.S. Dept of Commerce, Bureau of Economic Analysis

Table 7: Total Education Spending by Levels of Government in the U.S., Page 85 (Chantrill 2011)

Table 8: K-12 Education Spending by Levels of Government in the U.S., Page 86 (Chantrill 2011)